Organisations
with Soul

Hawthorn Press

Organisations with Soul copyright © 2013 Adriaan Bekman

First published in the Netherlands in 2011 by Uitgeverij Christofoor, Zeist under the title *De Taal van de Ziel* © 2011

Adriaan Bekman is hereby identified as the author of this work in accordance with section 77 of the Copyright, Designs and Patent Act, 1988. He asserts and gives notice of her moral right under this Act.

Published by Hawthorn Press, Hawthorn House,
1, Lansdown Lane, Stroud, Gloucestershire, GL5 1BJ, UK
www.hawthornpress.com

All rights reserved. No part of this book may be reproduced, stored in a retrieval system or transmitted in any form by any means (electronic or mechanical, through reprography, digital transmission, recording or otherwise) without prior written permission of the publisher.

English language Edition Organisations with Soul copyright © Hawthorn Press 2013
Cover illustration and illustrations © Adriaan Bekman
Typesetting and Cover design by Lucy Guenot
Translated by Philip Mees
Printed by Henry Ling Ltd, Dorset

The views expressed in this book are not necessarily those of the publisher.

British Library Cataloguing in Publication Data applied for

ISBN 978-1-907359-30-9

Organisations *with Soul*

A social path of schooling in the language of the human soul

Adriaan Bekman

Hawthorn Press

CONTENTS

Foreword ... 6

PART I
THE LANGUAGE OF THE SOUL

Introduction ... 12

The Soul's Origin
1. STARRY SKY – NATURE – EARTH FIRE ... 14
2. SPIRIT – SOUL – BODY ... 17
3. FAITH – HOPE – LOVE ... 19
4. THINKING – FEELING – WILL ... 21
5. MEMORY – LANGUAGE – CONSCIENCE ... 24
6. LIBERTY – EQUALITY – FRATERNITY ... 26
7. FATHER – SON – SPIRIT ... 28

The Soul in the Here and Now
8. BIOGRAPHY – DIALOGUE – PROCESS ... 30
9. LEADERSHIP – COMMUNITY – MEANING ... 33
10. ATTENTION – CONNECTION – TRUST ... 36
11. CONCENTRATION – POSITIVITY – DIRECTION ... 38
12. KNOWLEDGE – SKILL – ATTITUDE ... 40
13. IMAGINATION – EXPERIENCE – ACTION ... 42
14. IMAGE – JUDGEMENT – DECISION ... 44

The Soul Overcomes her Barriers and Creates her Future
15. TAKING – GIVING – SHARING ... 46
16. KEEPING ONE'S WORD – ENCOUNTERING – ACTING ... 49
17. HAPPINESS – RESIGNATION – SORROW ... 51
18. OBJECTS – RELATIONSHIP – COMMUNITY ... 54
19. HATE – GUILT – FEAR ... 56
20. DISTANCING – AVERSION – RESISTANCE ... 58
21. CONFIRMATION – MOVEMENT – CHANGE ... 60

Conclusion of Part 1 ... 62

PART 2
The Schooling of the Soul

Introduction	64
Paths of Schooling	67
The Basis for the Path of Schooling in the Social Realm	69
LIVING WITH A QUESTION	71
LIVING IN A PROCESS	77
LIVING IN DIALOGUE	85
LIVING IN ONE'S OWN BIOGRAPHY	91
The Context of the Path of Schooling in the Social Realm	94
LIVING IN ORGANISATIONS	96
LIVING IN ROLES	100
LIVING IN LEADERSHIP	103
LIVING IN THE SOUL	107
The Path of Schooling of Body, Soul and Spirit	110
The Personal Social Path to Higher Consciousness	118
Afterword	120
About the author	121
Bibliography	123

Foreword

Adriaan Bekman

This book researches the soul, that wonderful, old-fashioned word, soul. How did such a familiar word in common usage fall into disuse?

A possible cause of our forgetting the soul is the fact that we spend much of our lives in organisations. While in former times the human being lived in personal relationships and communities, and had immediate experiences there of life and death, survival and faith, today we are embedded in a web of self-organised life relationships that are mostly functionally and materially determined. In these functionally organised connections we create a world of our own with things, and also with meaning. These can only last if we take care of them ourselves. There here is little attention paid to people's inner world and experience. But it is exactly in this inner world that meaning and development occur, which enable us to take another step in our own growth. Our organised, functional world has, in my opinion, an urgent need of re-imagining with soul. The questions that we personally struggle with may not find new answers if we cannot find a new, conscious relationship to the human soul, especially in work situations where we are oriented toward results and production.

This is the message of this book.

This book offers an inquiry into the human soul in such a way that the soul, as a meaningful idea, can make a transformative entry into our organised human and personal life. This is especially important since in our society we are now confronted with unsolvable problems of our creation. These problems – such as the threats to our earth, hunger, war and violence, human suffering, dislocation, division, burn-out – work in the soul, and can ultimately only find responses from ourselves. Our striving for a perfectly functioning earth community continually runs aground on the rocks of its opposite.

It would be a good thing if we could be able to create a new, conscious relationship with our own soul. (This is part one)

Human beings can enter on a path of schooling to realise this,

I will give attention in part two to a path of schooling for the soul that is oriented toward schooling through other people, in other words, a schooling of consciousness in relationship with the other person.

In the long tradition of paths of schooling the focus usually was, and is, on the individual schooling of one's own soul. This is a meditative path with the objective of raising the soul to a higher level of consciousness. Here however, I want to sketch a path of schooling in social life. This is a more horizontal path that we can take and which, of course, can be strengthened by the more vertical, meditative individual path of schooling. This social path of schooling can especially help us in dealing with the problems of this time.

The premise: the human soul as paradox

In our inquiry into the human soul, her language and schooling, we choose as our premise the fact that the soul is a paradoxical reality. The human soul is potentially the space, the organ, within which our personal development takes place. We form our soul in the course of the path of development we travel personally in everyday life. So I would like to characterise the human soul as follows.

The created world in which we find ourselves – nature and cosmos – is harmonious. All things relate to each other. Sun, moon and earth have their orbits. The plant grows, the air is there. Our human spirit and body are embedded in this harmony. Our heart beats, our skin breathes, we live our life every day. Everything exists with everything in organic relationships.

There is only one exception – *the human soul*. Arthur Koestler describes this beautifully when he indicates that we can predict with great precision where the star Sirius will stand in the cosmos a million years from now, but that he is incapable of predicting with precision where his cook will be in five minutes. (Arthur Koestler: *Fruehe Empoerung, Limes Munchen*) We experience this every time when our feet have a mind of their own. We experience this when we have a different understanding from what the other person meant to say

It is this human soul which is created by us, and we do this out of our individual 'I' as 'I' spirit, together with the body in which we are dwelling. The soul, in its unique character, makes itself known and shows itself first of all in our thinking, feeling and will- these are the primary expressions of the soul.

With its self-created soul, the individual 'I' can break through and transcend natural and cosmic relationships. Aristotle already showed this to us in his economic writing, in which he describes how the human being – originally completely embedded in the organic, divine creation – breaks through the boundaries of nature. This began with barter, with the postponement of wants and needs, with the contemplation of the effects of an action. We leave our family, we travel the world, we do different work than our parents, we live with people that have different religions and values. We have entered an organised life that gives us a sense of ourselves. This breaking through boundaries also can go to extremes like abortion and euthanasia.

The long process of creating soul has given us, step by step, an individual consciousness that expresses itself in the way we express ourselves, the way we deal with each other, the way we meet the moral issues of our time. The memory we have and that we build up during life is an expression of the soul life. The language we share is an expression of soul life. The moral consciousness is an expression of the soul life. These three expressions become more and more individual and are connected to the personality we become.

The process of breaking through boundaries and 'begetting soul' thus becomes visible in human capacities such as memory, language and conscience. They are the carriers of our individual consciousness.

Everything the human soul touches on earth changes from a harmonious, organic order into paradoxical, contradictory relationships. In those relationships there is no longer any self-evident, organic principle at work. It is the human soul herself that is working there. In lieu of being harmonious, the world we create ourselves becomes paradoxical, a contradiction in itself.

Everything created by humans becomes a problem

The consequences of the paradoxical human creation are:
> Nothing of our own creation lasts all by itself
> Everything must bemaintained by us.
> Nothing of our own creation has meaning in and of itself.
> We have to add meaning.

This is in contrast to the natural world that we see around us and of which we are a part, which is objective and true. It exists by itself and has its own intsrinsic meaning and qualities.

The lasting existence and meaning of that which has been touched by human beings can only come about if human beings themselves create a process through which they ensure that:
> What was self-created will last, and
> Meaning is added to what was self-created.

As a result, the human being is chained to his or her own creations. These continually call to us to:
> Care for me, make me last;
> Give me meaning.

Increasingly we see a paradoxical world appear on earth, created by human beings. It is the world of problems, of 'dis-relationships' and of disconnection
How does this paradoxical character come to expression? Some examples include:
> It is not self-evident that someone will do what he said he would do;
> It is not self-evident that when one speaks the other listens;

It is not self-evident that a house, once built, maintains itself;
It is not self-evident that a quality system, once created, works by itself;
That the novel, once written, has meaning only when it is read;
That students learn in lectures and seminars;
That the hotel comes to life when there are guests;
That a service is performed when it is paid for;
That the car moves if we drive it.

Summary

So we can say that the human spirit, our 'I', in interaction with the human body, creates and forms a soul dwelling This becomes visible in the processes in which we live and which we (work?) carry into effect. Human creation arises from this, but we also develop our own consciousness. Our thinking, feeling and will develop themselves as fundamental soul forces. We develop structured thinking, 'lived' feeling and a moral, active will when we are willing to embark on a path of schooling the soul. This path is the path of the modern organised life, the exploration of the new community that comes forward out of the social and economic life we live in today. Here we meet our companions that travel with us during all our life and who are the soul mates leading us to a higher consciousness of life and the forces beyond the life we live.

To summarise, I will explore the following questions in this book:

Part 1: What is 'the language of the soul'. How does the soul express herself, how does she manifest herself?

In Part 2, I will inquire into 'the schooling of the soul'. I will describe a social path of schooling of the soul in everyday life, a path that is different from the individual path of schooling through meditation.

PART 1

THE LANGUAGE OF THE SOUL

Introduction

In our personal lives we use a language of the soul to express what lives in our inner world. For instance, you can tell your partner or child that you love them. They will not be startled to hear it, and in most cases will receive it gratefully.

In our life in organisations, as member of staff or client, this is not obvious. It would be unusual and probably unprofessional to tell your manager you love him. In organisations there is no generally accepted soul language with which you can express your inner world. A functional or informational language reigns there, for expressing external things. Words such as goals, strategy, problem, approach, system and structure are used. Words such as love, fear, trust, or relate are not used as a matter of course in an organisational context.

In my enquiries into a potential language of the soul in organisations, I came up with twenty-one soul 'triads' which I describe and characterise below. After every description of a triad I will ask a question for inner reflection, which can help readers embark on their own investigation into soul language in organisational contexts. As an illustration I will also give an example from my own life practice.

The Soul's Origin

The first series of seven triads leads us into the history of the soul, the 'begetting of soul' in human community.

The Soul in the Here and Now

The second series of seven triads takes us into the soul's contemporary actuality, giving us reference points for consciously experiencing our own soul language.

The Soul Overcomes her Barriers and Creates Her Future

The third series of seven triads highlights expressions of the soul which we need to learn to deal with since they dominate our lives.

These twenty-one triads offer us a language of the soul for expressing inner worlds. Considerations, feelings and intentions reign in these inner worlds, and largely determine what manifests outwardly. If we become capable of developing an eye and an ear for these, and expressing them, we will greatly enrich organisational life and, in addition, give ourselves a solid foundation for expressing judgements and decisions that form and inform our lives.

The Soul's Origin

The first seven triads present images of the origin of the soul. The soul can be viewed as a creative deed of higher beings, and yet at the same time as the transformation of harmonious existence into paradoxical reality.

The soul thus acquired the potential to be human, and in our life here on earth we develop this capacity into an experience of reality. Within the soul we can assert our individuality.

1 STARRY SKY – NATURE – EARTH FIRE

Our human existence is enacted here on this planet and unfolds between heaven and earth. From time immemorial the meaning of our life on earth has been viewed in terms of a future eternal life in heaven, towards which the soul is journeying. Divine creative power has put us here on earth. That is the picture of the created soul. Placed first in an earthly paradise, but then expelled from it, this earth proved to be the portal to a completely different existence, of labour and travail, and of tempering in the fire of experience.

The story of this evolving human being is told repeatedly in different cultures. It seems to be our fate, living between starry sky and earth fire, to have a hand in our own development rather than being merely pre-ordained. How do we, as human beings within the natural world, find our own path between heaven and earth?

The human being comes to earth from a heavenly world. On earth we are born out of nature and live a natural life until death. History reveals not only the good but also the destructive sides of human nature. Human life takes place not only in nature, but also in a moral domain. As human beings we have, or can have, responsibility of our own, making our own ethical choices.

This dilemma of both a natural and a moral existence has been experienced by people through the ages, and has been described in all of humanity's stories. Examples are the fairytales of the Brothers Grimm, the

Old and New Testament, the Kalevala, the stories of a Thousand and One Nights, the Koran, and the Bhagavad Gita. But every novel or film relates a similar story. These stories show that human life always encounters the question of being young and growing old, of crisis and catharsis, a happy outcome or an unhappy one, of growth and decay.

The human being standing between heaven and earth is a good, original picture of the soul: between the starry sky above us and the immense forces of fire below us, we seek our own, self-created equilibrium.

Humanity originally focused on the cosmic heavenly world above as its primary orientation. Astrology was the prevailing science, while faith was the all-powerful force that gave meaning to everything.

After many thousands of years human beings shifted their orientation to the immeasurable forces below them in the earth. In the earth are found the raw materials that have made our economic existence possible. From agriculture and hunting in nature we have turned to exploitation of the earth's resources. Technology arose as a system that seeks to control everything and keep its grip on the 'earth fire'. This newer science, of nature and earth, now dominates our worldview. Chained to the earth, we strive for a long, materially prosperous existence with the aid of science and technology. We have lost sight of the starry world. Spirit and cosmos are now very distant. Only when confronted by death do we feel a connection again with this lost world of heaven, the world in which the soul originates.

Question for inner reflection

I have described the soul as embedded in a natural existence, living between starry sky and earth fire. I have also described the soul as living within an historical narrative: a world of good and evil, a moral world.

> *In the practice of your daily life, what is your relationship to these two worlds of the soul, the natural world and the moral?*

Example

In the daily practice of my work I am continually confronted with my clients' practical and moral questions. It is my intention, and I try, to help them with these questions so that they can nurture their organisations, and take developmental steps. There are also times when I pull back and devote myself to the natural world – the soul nourishment of my little Irish cottage by a river. There I reflect on what I am so busy with. I come to myself, to inner quiet.

2 SPIRIT – SOUL – BODY

We walk around on the earth in a body, which is central to our human existence. The body is our dwelling place, and we have proved to be increasingly capable of prolonging the span of its life, of living to an ever more advanced age. It is thought that future generations may think of 100 as a normal life expectancy. Some scientists even predict that we will eventually be able to make our body a permanent dwelling place. We remain on earth. We feed the body, we take care of it, we heal it. We dwell in that body.

In the body lives the human spirit which expresses itself in the 'I'. This 'I' inhabits the body. The human spirit incarnates in the body. Body and spirit are two opposite poles of Creation.

Body and spirit can both be developed and cared for. They can also be neglected and destroyed. The body is emphatically present. The spirit, however, must be called, awoken.

The body is connected with nature. It is part of a natural world which arises and perishes, but always returns cyclically. Nature is self-evident in this sense. It comes into being out of its own lawfulness. We can experience this in the beating of our heart, the sweat on our skin, in our breathing in and breathing out, in the flow of our blood. We are awake and we sleep, we grow and age. We fall ill and recover.

For those who acknowledge the reality of the spirit, it is born from a divine spiritual world. The human spirit is a being that knows itself to be part of the invisible world of God. We can experience a reflection of this in our dreams and imagination. I am part of humanity, but there is no one like me. I am a unique individual in a sea of humanity. In every dream reigns the uniquely individual, but also the archetypal. For the spirit, there is always both the 'I' and the 'whole'.

The human soul is related to both, but is neither. She is, above all, the human being's creative deed. The soul comes into being, is formed, not as a fixed given but a potential, a possibility. The soul is a space that can be occupied, a melody that can be sung, an image that can be thought, an inspiring encounter, a purposeful deed.

The human soul has fallen out of Creation. She has developed inner contradictions, has become detached from the harmonious, cosmic world of nature. We raise our own soul, and in that soul we raise ourselves. The soul is an entity in the process of becoming, and it is the only entity through which we as human beings are able to work in a creative way.

Out of our human soul we create our own world. We surround ourselves with a material world, an organised world of products and services. We also create an inner world of our own in which we can live, and which makes it possible for us to relate in our own way to all that is in us and around us.

Question for inner reflection

I have described our dwelling place as body and spirit. Those have been given to us. We ourselves, on the other hand, must develop the soul. Whereas body and spirit were formed in harmony, the soul is a paradox.

> *How do you experience this soul world of contradictions in yourself?*
> *What effects does this have on the body?*
> *How do you navigate there with your own 'I'?*

Example

As a result of too much stress my body developed a chronic infection. Good medical treatment coupled with movement exercises helped overcome the infection. I now always look for balance between exertion and relaxation, action and reflection, between caring for and challenging body and spirit. In this way I am slowly developing antennae for my healthy state of soul equilibrium.

3 FAITH – HOPE – LOVE

The human soul has fallen out of a unified Creation, both natural and divine, and has incarnated into the seemingly godless, inhospitable land of earth. Helpless and hopeless, the soul has been left to its own fate: to inhabit its created world. As human beings, how can we recreate by our own powers a connection with this divine-natural spirit of Creation?

The first bridge we can build is faith – which expresses a religious connection between the human being and his origins. Faith is a soul condition in which we create contact with our Creator. It is expressed in ritual, sacramental acts, in liturgical gestures, in prayer or meditation. In reconnecting with our origin in this way, we can develop a deeply rooted awareness of our essential nature, expressed in the words 'I am'.

Religious consciousness gives us an experience of blessing and mercy in our existence, in our soul being.

But the soul cannot exist merely in faith. She finds herself in the darkness of this perplexing earth existence, on her way to a destination of which we have no sure knowledge. This realisation shows itself in hope. One day, as we hope, the soul will return to the home of our Creator, and will be born anew in that spiritual world.

The soul, having left her home and arrived in seemingly godless earth existence, finds herself facing the question of where we come from and where we are going. Her light is her own. The soul carries her own lamp as she seeks to return to divine existence, to be made one again with spirit and nature; she searches for ultimate harmony.

Out of this contradiction, this confrontation, this incapacity, the soul lives in hope. Hope is an active soul force that enables us to learn to see the future and make it possible.

Faith and hope wane and fade if they are not filled with love. The power of love creates soul warmth. It is connected with the heartbeat. Caught up in godless egotism, the struggle for survival, bare existence, we nevertheless seek love to flower within us. It is the other who kindles the spark for this love, the victory over our own egotism. The loving deed which responds to the need of the other brings the soul into an exalted state of being. With love we pull ourselves out of our own morass, bridging contradictions and creating human harmony. Love can become an all-pervading soul power that transforms us human beings into humanity, brings us together and imbues our faith and hope with warmth.

Question for inner reflection

Through faith in our origins, hope in the future, and love in the here and now, we overcome our egotism.

> *What roles do faith, hope and love play in your life?*
> *Can you think of good examples?*

Example

In my work with clients I am expected to give them my attention. But time and again I notice that I am thinking too much of my own processes and ideas. Redirecting my attention to my client's story, making his hope for the future explicit in our dialogue, and walking lovingly by his side – even when the path is not clear – is exactly how I find my own next step. I then discover new insight into my own questions, or can let go of an idea I had been holding on to.

4 THINKING – FEELING – WILL

The soul develops specific forms within us. She manifests in our thinking, feeling and will.

Thinking

Thoughts are constantly coursing through us. For instance, we reflect on what has just occurred to us. These thoughts give meaning to our existence. Thinking is a soul activity, bringing movement into the world of ideas. It explores the world of creative powers which reveal themselves in ideas. The soul can internalise an idea and ripen it to maturity. She elaborates the idea into her own thought. Thinking is like a drill that enables us to penetrate the invisible world of the spirit. Through thinking we create clarity in the obscure world of meaning. Thinking is a light that shines in the invisible space of consciousness.

I remember in my sociology studies being confronted with new theories and concepts. By reading attentively, and in discussions with other students, sometimes something would suddenly dawn on me. 'Aha, is that how it is.' When I stop and think about incomprehensible personal experiences I may suddenly see a light in the distance; I may suddenly recognise the meaning of the experience.

Feeling

The soul can also show and experience herself in our feelings. These come and go, filling us and giving value to what happens to us or to what we accomplish. Feelings can be powerful and carry us away. But they can also be subtle and fine. Our feelings bring our experiences to life in us. These experiences enter us through feelings. They can be explosive and will often show up in our facial and bodily expression. Thus I am able to observe when someone is irritated or hurt, angry or relieved, interested or bored. In this way our feelings can become a sense organ with which we explore the other. Feelings can be shared.

An encounter with someone may unleash all kinds of feelings in me. Sometimes they tumble over each other in their rush to come out. Afterwards, after a number of meetings with this person, a kind of basic mood will grow, perhaps one of challenge, or perhaps one that affirms me. This basic mood is there every time I meet this person. It enables me to observe better through my feelings what is going on in the other so that I can meet him or her in a more effective manner.

Will

The will is a force that lives deep in our subconscious. Incentives and motives stimulate us to action, impulses bring us into movement. Through a deed we intervene in the world and, for a moment at least, we put our stamp on the world. Our deeds may have decisive effects on our lives but also on the lives of others. Here we find ourselves in the realm of morality. Good and evil live here – doing what is right or making mistakes.

For instance, I feel called to take an initiative and invite others to join me. Some of them join, others don't. We make a step and right away we call forth reactions on the part of others. These may distract us, or they may help us along.

When we school our thinking and rise to a higher quality of consciousness, we can enable our soul to refine our feelings and to transform our deeds into positive actions through this higher kind of thinking. Consciously reflecting on our relationship to the other, and our deeds *vis-à-vis* the other, grows into meaningful patterns that will last. We overcome superficiality of encounter, arbitrariness of feelings, and repeatedly postponed actions by taking a step together with the other, so that our question grows, our insight is deepened, our connection is strengthened. While all we do and are comes and goes, is born and dies, the soul that consciously thinks, refines and permeates feeling, and expresses will creatively, forms her own spiritual substance which can find permanent existence in the world of spirit.

Question for inner reflection

I have described how conscious thinking enables us to refine and direct our impulses of feeling and will. We enter into a conscious connection with the other and make a conscious step forward.

> *How do you strengthen your thinking?*
> *And what is the effect of that on your feeling and will life?*

Example

For many years I have schooled myself in writing texts, playing music, and drawing and painting biographical situations. I sometimes succeed in creating something in word, image or sound that helps someone with a fundamental question of their own.

5   MEMORY – LANGUAGE – CONSCIENCE

The human soul is in a process of becoming that manifests in her developing thinking, feeling and will. This development can be observed in metamorphosis and intensification. The soul transforms herself towards higher levels of consciousness. The soul also wants to become more and more real and tangible. In the history of humanity the soul is working towards her own revelation. We are living in this soul revelation. How does this become apparent?

The soul becomes specific and real in our memory. Living in the here and now, between past and future, the soul builds up an internalised memory. Again and again we can call up in our memory what has taken place in ourselves and work inwardly on what we have thus called up. In this way we sharpen our practical life into valuable memories. And these memories build a soul construct in which we can express ourselves to others. We can share these memories with each other; we can tell them to each other.

For this purpose the soul has developed language. Out of a world of creative sound, human beings have distilled a language of their own. In this human language, observation and idea come together. We bring our reflections to life in words and concepts, and thus we communicate with each other. In childhood we acquire a mother tongue. Based on this foundation we can also develop a professional language, a scientific language, or an intimate language.

We transform the events in our lives in our conscience. Our lives and our souls are not meaningless, but our individual conscience creates a bridge between the lives we lead and the universal values that we seek to guide us. Our conscience develops into a guiding star that accompanies our soul on her path of development.

Our conscience actively directs our soul to qualities in our lives. It brings us to a level of consciousness where questions can live which we ask of ourselves, of our souls. Conscience thus becomes a voice that accompanies us and that always and in everything wants to speak to us and question us.

Our soul constantly tries to escape from this voice of conscience. She clings to ideologies, supposed truths, immoral longings and white lies. Our conscience connects us with the universal world of human values in which the soul and her work can be reflected. The soul is at her most beautiful when she makes room for the voice of conscience.

Question for inner reflection

The soul manifests in a process of metamorphosis and intensification, in which memory, language and conscience develop.

> How do you deal with your memories, how do you share them with others? How do you listen to the voice of your conscience?

Example

I am often asked to give a lecture or workshop. Almost always I accept such invitations. I carry them around in my head and think about them now and then until the day arrives. Only then do I decide what to do and what to say. When I meet the people the accent is going to shift anyway from what I had prepared beforehand. I make very sure that what I am saying is solidly anchored in my own life experience.

6 LIBERTY – EQUALITY – FRATERNITY

The soul has fallen out of the divine world and has found herself in her own creative space. The human soul is at home in spirit and nature, in physical qualities we share with soil, plant, animal, and with water, air and warmth. She is also moved by spirit, by creative beings who offer us their spiritual work as dwelling place. But the soul also stands on her own and engages with what is uniquely human.

The soul can stand autonomously within her own nature because the human being has the capacity for freedom. In her paradoxical reality, the soul can create her own composition, can tell her own story, can perform her own deed in freedom. Freedom is the unique human quality, which is unknown to any other being above or below us. In astonishment we can experience and take into ourselves this cosmos of our own, and this freedom. Our soul bears her own responsibility and can integrate the harvest of life into her own essential being.

This freedom as potential of the human soul here on earth is accompanied by the potential to break away from hierarchical relationships. We do not necessarily need to stand above or below. We have the gods and nature beside us. We do not need to make ourselves subservient to what a higher hierarchy of angels, archangels and other creative beings gives to us. We also do not need to make ourselves superior to what has been given to us on earth. We can respectfully and in equality be part of, and work with, all that lives in and around us.

The fundamental qualities of our soul also appear in our ability to serve others. We can wash the feet of the other, feed and clothe the other, take care of him and cherish him, school him and love him. We can be brothers and sisters who want to enter into a common destiny with each other. We can become humanity.

Liberty, equality and fraternity are the soul ideals through which we can progress ever further. Nature does not supply them: we ourselves must realise them. When we gain insight into ourselves in conscious self-reflection, when our soul becomes the mirror of our entire existence, these three ideals can come into being as beacons of human existence. Especially if we accept all that makes us different from one another as our own creative space, and if we learn to work with that, then these exclusively human ideals will rise up among us as life principles which advance our humanity.

Question for inner reflection

These three human soul values distinguish us from the rest of nature: freedom in our thinking, equality in our relationships with others, and brotherly service performed for another out of love for his existence.

> *How do you live with these human values of liberty, equality and fraternity in the daily practice of your work? What roles do your customer, your colleague, your customer play here, and how important are their roles?*

Example

I make sure that in my work with a client I am completely available for as long as I am there. I do not allow other questions to disturb me. I work together with colleagues and I strive to do that in equality and by making use of everyone's special capacities. It is great when that works. I strive to develop a critical view of my own thoughts, and to internalise ideas which can give form to my contribution to society and make it accessible to others.

7 FATHER – SON – SPIRIT

The human soul originates from the primeval all. Expelled from Paradise, she lost contact with the source, and knowledge of her deeper purpose. The human soul is a wanderer, has lost her way and has attached herself to what was cast off, what has fallen. The human soul can't make it on her own. She needs a beacon to orient herself.

The soul has her origin in the Father. The Father is the source from which everything has sprung. Whether you believe we descended from ape or angel, the soul can always turn to the Father. We can meet the Father when we retrace our way back to our origins, in our parents and grandparents, in nature as we find it, in our spirit, in all the living beings surrounding us.

The soul, however, is not naturally at home in the world of the Father; she is no longer completely secure in heredity and origin.

The soul also encounters the Son. She goes through ups and downs, experiences crisis. The soul breaks through natural boundaries and encounters unknown forces in unknown worlds. The soul is capable of sacrifice: through the Son she can have a healing and restorative effect on other souls. The soul can hold back her own inner being and create a space for the soul development of the other.

When in this way the soul undergoes a process of dying and being reborn, her own spirit, the higher 'I' can arise in her. This 'I' seeks the spirit that enables the soul to be born. The spirit brings together human beings who are totally different from each other. It is the spirit that enables one 'I' speak to another.

Thus the soul 'stands up' when she seeks her origins and does not allow herself to be permanently lost. The soul stands up when she connects with the life process of dying and becoming, always getting up again and taking the next step. The soul stands up when she invokes the spirit in the other, when she awakens the 'I' of the other.

Father, Son and Spirit are the beacons for the soul on her path of development, as she makes her way through darkness and unknowing.

Question for inner reflection

The soul can be guided by beacons: the Father as the source of being, the Son as the process of self-becoming, and the Spirit as the power of 'I'-awakening to the other and in oneself.

> *How do you address the other? Do you address his difficulty or instead the 'I' that has to cope with that hindrance? Can you view the other as involved in a developmental process, with the Father standing behind him in the background?*

Example

As Chairman of the Board of Trustees of a large institute for children with special needs I have been deeply impressed with the way staff make efforts to address the children with infinite patience, focusing on the 'I' that is concealed behind developmental difficulty. They attempt to do this out of their own 'I' power. Whenever that 'I' of the child makes its appearance, the sun breaks through and the child makes a step forward. Something becomes possible that could not be done before.

The Soul in the Here and Now

The next seven triads describe the soul in her actual existence in the here and now. We experience the soul in a dual way: we are embedded in what nature and spirit bestow on us, and this connects us with the weft of Creation. Yet at the same time we also live within our own creations, our organised and self-determining existence.

While family, nation or religion may provide us with an experience of natural relationships and creative powers, for instance in begetting and raising our children, this is no longer a given where we experience our isolated individuality. There, it can seem, we live in a temporal world, a world of senselessness, in which we can only survive if we develop the soul into a creative organ that gives meaning to things.

The next seven triads speak of creating meaning in the life we lead in our self-organizing existence.

8 BIOGRAPHY – DIALOGUE – PROCESS

The soul appears in the human biography, our life story. The human biography is a composition of the complex being that we are, arising from the hereditary roots of parents and ancestors. It is reflected in our genes. But it is also formed during our life by the surroundings in which we live. The prevailing culture moulds us in the way we are brought up, the education we receive, the practical things we learn from people around us, our profession and job. Our surroundings inscribe themselves in us.

At the same time, the human being is a unique personality not identical with anyone else. We are a separate 'I' which takes up its stance within heredity and environment, and can become visible as an authentic entity. In our lives we encounter our own destiny, our 'karma', and must face self-invoked joys, trials and tribulations.

This biographical life process takes place as the fruit of all life processes in which the soul lives. From birth we engage in life processes. We eat and drink, wash and dress ourselves; we learn, work and travel; we fight and we love. The soul journeys through many parallel processes that repeat themselves rhythmically over and over again. Events occur which our soul must absorb and process, giving rise to our soul substance.

In these processes we are not alone but are in constant dialogue with others. We meet and influence each other. We accompany each other and take our leave again. We do this in a variety of different relationships with each other: as supplier and customer, teacher and student, producer and consumer, service provider and service purchaser. We also meet as members of the same community. We share family, town, country, church, club, business.

In these many processes the soul undergoes a constant flow of experiences and perceptions and can wake up in them. While we more or less sleep through things to begin with, as we grow older the soul can undergo a process of increasing awakening and gain in depth. She can transcend the boundaries and obstacles she encounters. She can explore unknown worlds. Thus she writes with her finger in the sand of natural creation, shaping her own life story in a way that may inspire others. The soul can become a guiding star that others will want to follow. Souls can guide and support each other through life in the steps they take on their path of development.

Question for inner reflection

Here biography appears as the all-encompassing life story in which heredity, education and also the individual 'I' inscribe themselves. We live through this biography in dialogue with others.

> How has your biography developed in dialogue with people who are important to you whether blood relatives, teachers or those who have made a mark on your life in some way? Have you had important encounters that influenced you or altered the course of your life? What life processes play a part in your life, and how do you nurture these?

Example

From my parents I learned to brush my teeth before going to bed. Back and forth with that brush. In military service I was taught: Up and down with that brush. When I started getting serious cavities between my teeth, my dentist taught me to brush between the teeth. Later still I learned to work with an electric brush. The simple process of brushing teeth developed and altered during my biography.

I can also describe more profound work processes which formed me in the independent institute in which I collaborated for twenty-eight years with some twenty colleagues, where I collaborated on a common impulse that we wanted to introduce into the world.

Father　　　　　Son　　　　　Spirit

Attention   Connection   Trust

Anxiety   Hate   Responsibility

Confirmation   Movement   Change

Biography   Dialogue   Process

Training of the Soul

Living in a Process

Dialogue

The Biography

Living in Organisations

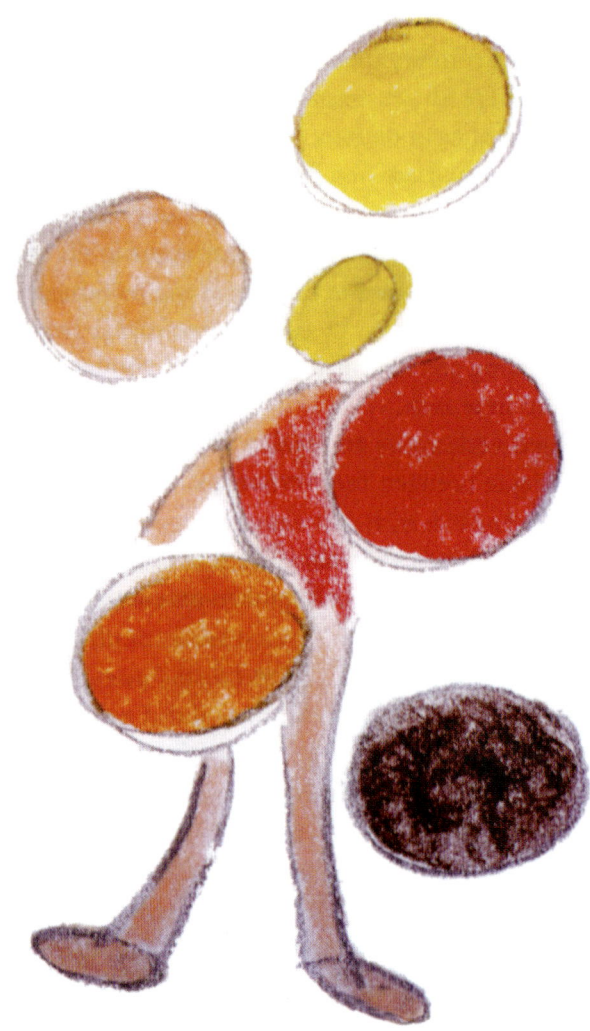

Living in Roles

Living in Leadership

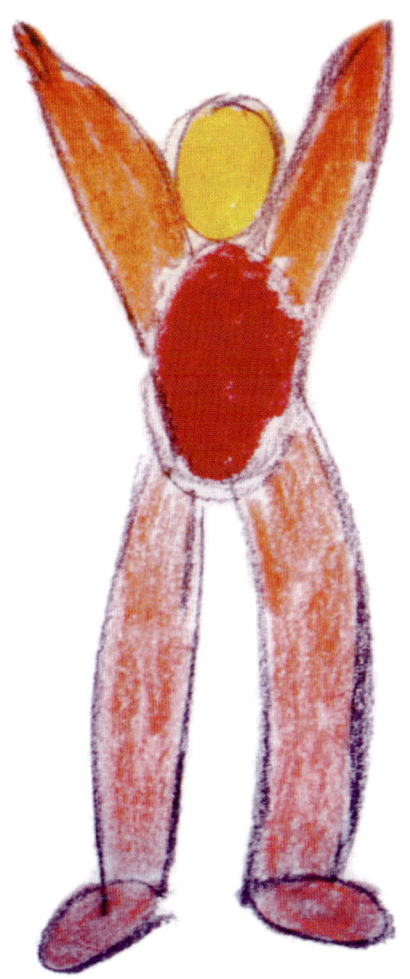

9 LEADERSHIP – COMMUNITY – MEANING

To begin with, the soul is guided by the hereditary and spirit-forming forces in which she is born. As time goes on, our own 'I', our individual spirit, can gradually take the lead in unfolding its own soul development. In this way the soul emancipates herself from these hereditary and spirit-forming forces and develops a level of being that is intrinsic to her alone. The son does not become like the father, nor the daughter like the mother: they become different and will stand on their own feet.

To some extent we choose and determine the course of our own life, make individual choices. Such choices also becomes visible in the professional training we embark on, and the responsible, professional dialogue we enter into with others.

At first we see the soul as a creation that comes into being from the work others have performed on it. Gradually the soul then arrives in her own creative space: everything she herself realises and enacts through hand, heart and head. In this creative space of her own, the soul meets and enters into dialogue with the other. This creates a horizontal space between two souls, one solely occupied by what these souls share with each other. For instance, when two people have a conversation and engage with each other, a common soul space will grow in which they can live together. This horizontal space between two people is opened by the question which one asks of the other. It is the 'Parsifal motif'. What does that mean?

The key element in the Parsifal story is the encounter of two individuals, one of whom is suffering. The other, Parsifal, observes this person's suffering, but initially fails to engage with this suffering by asking what ails him. The Parsifal story shows us how a soul who has become conscious can address the other soul in her suffering and is then able to bring a healing process into motion. Perception of what the other is suffering, and the act of asking the healing question, enables the other's soul to develop.

In this way the human being enters into community with others: 'I' and 'you'. Through orientation towards the other, through giving the other an impulse for soul development by asking a healing question, our own soul too is opened so that, discovered through the other, something new can enter.

Soul development takes place in community; it happens through dialogue with other people. Thus, as human beings we create new realities in dialogue with each other. These self-created soul realities, however, unlike what is naturally given us, do not endure on their own. They are lost if we do not maintain them ourselves. Thus we see that the buildings we construct wear down if we do not maintain them; that a system we create will only continue to work if we take care of it; that a decision is only transformed into deed if everyone also decides to do this; that a relationship will only last if it is nurtured. In addition, these realities have meaning only if the soul constantly adds new meaning to them.

Such meaning does not arise directly out of asking the healing question, the question that brings the other into motion. Meaning must be created out of an inner effort for conscious comprehension. To this end, we need to undertake our own explorations into meaningful ideas by asking a conceptual question aimed at the understanding of an idea, and by working with this idea. Because the soul is also occupied with fundamental spiritual and religious themes, sensitivity and insight will arise in the process. This creates meaning in the soul. We can do this, for instance, through meditation, study or spiritual research.

When we make a connection between the healing question we ask of the other and the conceptual exploration of a meaningful idea, new soul substance arises in us. The soul becomes seeing; she is filled with meaning.

This creates a force of attraction felt by other souls. We are all familiar with encounters with a creative impulse that has inspired our own soul. Be it a book, a film, or a person's initiative and work, our soul can be attracted by the soul of someone who created this work. Thus there can form a new community of connected souls who may not even have physically met each other.

Question for inner reflection

When we become active in society we enter into community with others. We can participate in shaping this community and contribute to the creation of its meaning by asking the healing question of others, and by immersing ourselves in spiritual content.

> *How do you become part of communities, and how do you take part in shaping them? How do you create meaning in life?*

Example

I participate in a worldwide community of people who are committed to organisational development, based both on individual self-development and community development. Every year over a hundred colleagues come together for a week to deepen this impulse, to undertake research together, and to encourage each other to introduce into their client organisations a human-scale developmental impulse.

10 ATTENTION – CONNECTION – TRUST

The power of attention works in the horizontal space between human souls. When we direct our attention to the situation in which we find ourselves, this will immediately initiate a development there in the realm of the soul. When we pay attention to something or someone, something is going to happen. This is true in the case of a mother and her child, a customer and his supplier, a manager and his colleague. In the many life situations in which the soul finds herself she is constantly confronted by the presence, or absence, of attention. To the extent that the soul is better able to live attentively, she will be a blessing to others.

Attention comes into being when our own 'I' takes charge in the soul. This immediately radiates soul warmth which will be noticed by the other. Through attention, the soul acknowledges the other person and whatever events are occurring. This creates the possibility for souls to connect with each other. The soul can enter into what is happening, into the process that is taking place, and also into what has to be done. The soul connects and remains present. The connected soul enables the process that is occurring to work. This will become a lasting connection when the soul can make the event or the process that is happening her own.

Thus a customer may give me a task. He expects me to be fully capable of executing it and gives his attention to something else. Later he may be surprised and disappointed in the result because it differs from what he had expected. However, if the customer monitors the task he has given me with positive personal attention, this will also help me to execute the task with personal attention, and to connect myself with the customer. In this way trust can arise between us.

When connections are made, trust grows between souls. Trust is a deep longing of the soul. Especially in our own creative endeavours, and most of all in the organisations we create, the longing for trust plays an important role, as does the experience of lack of trust. In organisations, different souls work together who would be unable to tolerate each other in natural communities. That is because there is a third factor at work: the customer or client. Without this third, collaboration would be difficult.

Attention to the customer creates connections and these, in turn, create trust. With trust you can move forward together into a creative relationship. Trust is nurtured when we often do things together with attention for the other and for the situation. Attention, connection and trust create a horizontal space between us in which the soul can make progress. That fills the human being with deep inner satisfaction. We come to ourselves, and to the self of the other.

Question for inner reflection

If the soul devotes herself to a task with attention she is able to connect with the task. Two people set out together. That creates a basis for mutual trust. In our work together we try not to betray this trust.

> *How do you direct your attention? To whom or to what do you give your attention? How do you connect with others around a task, and how do you create an atmosphere of trust in that process?*

Example

A new colleague in our institute wishes to get involved in work with customers. This process gets going, for instance, when I take her with me into customer situations and start working with her. In this way the new colleague gets involved. If she now also pays attention to me, and if she nurtures the relationship, the connection between us will become stronger and our mutual trust will grow.

11 CONCENTRATION – POSITIVITY – DIRECTION

The soul is willing to learn. Our 'I' can take the soul in hand and lead her on a path of schooling. From time immemorial, the soul has been taught and developed in schools and mystery centres, which have existed in all cultural epochs. Our educational system still reflects something of these ancient paths of schooling.

There is a teacher and there is a student. The student receives tasks which initiate the learning process, but he is also tested by the teacher on the results of his learning. The point of the tests is not only to measure knowledge but also the student's attitude, and to awaken his will to learn.

In order to strengthen the soul, the 'I' can invoke the power of concentration. In thinking, the soul focuses on a question, an observation, an experience, and penetrates these by concentration. The thoughts remain focused; they do not drift away. You just need to try that for a brief moment and all kinds of other thoughts will run through your head. Concentration means keeping your attention focused. This strengthens the soul's power of thinking.

The soul can focus on events and approach these in a positive way. We have the tendency to focus on what is negative, what has failed or frustrates us, while we often fail to notice what is good. Looking for the positive in everything does not mean being naively positive. The negative causes us to distance ourselves so that we remove ourselves both inwardly and outwardly. The positive leads us towards things: we come closer, and we can connect with what is there, even if it does not appear attractive.

Besides giving concentrated focus to our reality, besides connecting with this reality in a positive manner, we can also direct our will to take this reality in hand. As we saw above, what we ourselves initiate or create has the life and meaning we give to it. This demands a deed of will, a directed intervention. In such a deed we encounter resistance in ourselves and also from outside. We can overcome this resistance if our will is directed by what we consider important, but also if we direct our will to what is needed by the other. This is the free deed, respectfully orientated to the needs of the other.

When we strengthen our thinking through attentive concentration, our feeling through positive connection, and our will power through the free deed orientated to the need of the other, this activity of the 'I' strengthens the power of the soul to a level of consciousness at which we can master the most difficult questions, the most vexing processes we are involved in, the most demanding challenges we face.

Question for inner reflection

The soul strengthens herself by learning to concentrate her thinking, by directing her feelings in a positive way, and by strengthening will through free deeds. In this way we can strengthen the soul so that she can meet difficult challenges and prevail.

> *How do you strengthen your soul? Where do you direct your concentrated attention? How do you awaken positive feelings in situations that tend to bring about the opposite? How do you direct your will to what you consider important for you to do?*

Example

When I have written something I regularly read it through again. Sometimes I can be startled by what I read, and try to change it for the better. I wonder who I am writing this for, what it is I want to demonstrate, what are good examples so that the reader will understand what I want to say. Here concentrated thinking, a positive attitude and a clear will impetus go hand-in-hand. If your text touches someone when he reads it, your life gains meaning.

12 KNOWLEDGE – SKILL – ATTITUDE

The path of schooling the soul undertakes is enacted both in everyday practical life, in which she tries to participate consciously, and in inner reflection which we want to undertake in our personal schooling. The soul forms herself through these two aspects.

The soul acquires knowledge as a result of instruction by others but also, and increasingly, by generating knowledge of her own as fruits of the process of schooling. Knowledge also mirrors the stance and quality of the soul. Abstract knowledge shows a different soul quality than, for instance, artistic knowledge or knowledge gained in practical life. Knowledge that shows itself as the fruit of inner life is something others are able to accept. It is living knowledge. It is different when the soul wants to communicate knowledge she has not herself gained. This will be resisted by the soul of the other.

The soul also reveals herself in her skills, her abilities. Through exercises the soul can acquire real skills through ongoing practice. We say then that a person has a skill 'at his fingertips'. The soul likes to demonstrate such skills: constant engagement with the complexities of life invokes the soul's skill. Boundaries must be overcome in the schooling of skill. This is a process of backsliding and leaping forward again. When the soul shapes herself in and through developing a skill, this can have a productive effect on the situation and the process in which we are living and working.

Skills can be demonstrated in different qualities. We can develop technical manual skills, or social skills, or conceptual skills. We penetrate things with our entire being when we make these three skills our own in relation to a question or a process. We can observe this when we see a professional, who really understands his trade, serve his customer, when a musician performs for the public, or when a scientist shares his discovery with his colleagues.

The soul also reveals herself in her outlook, both in her own fundamental outlook and professional outlook. Outlook is a manner of being into which we gradually grow. We form our attitudes and outlook largely based on the behaviour and examples of others. We gradually adopt such attitudes more and more, and then clothe our appearance to others in them.

Knowledge, skill and outlook come together in the role we adopt in life which, in turn, brings out these three soul manifestations. Adopting a role is schooling for the soul. Staying in your role reinforces this schooling of the soul.

Question for inner reflection

When the soul develops and matures, this comes to expression in acquired knowledge, skills and in a fundamental attitude. It becomes visible in the way you work in your trade or profession. In the role you play, knowledge, skills and attitude make their appearance as realised soul.

> *How do you work in your trade or profession? How do you perform a role? Where do you excel, and how do others react to that?*

Example

My daughter one day asked me: 'What kind of work do you do?'

'I sit in rooms and have conversations with people,' was my first answer.

'What do you talk about?' she then asked.

'About their questions and how they can be good managers for others.'

'What do you know about that?' she asked with a smile.

'That is a question you should really ask my customers. After a conversation with me they do things a little differently and sometimes they are surprised to see the effect that has,' I replied, also with a smile.

Later, when she had seen me at work one day, she was proud of her father. 'You did that beautifully!'

13   IMAGINATION – EXPERIENCE – ACTION

The soul brings about tangible results. She transforms herself into tangible outcomes when she appears in the form of a specific picture or vision in my head. We generate imaginative pictures and thus create fixed images of the world for ourselves. The soul is an imagination of things. In these imaginations she relates observations and ideas or concepts to each other. These imaginations reflect the soul's quality of being. An imagination can become rigid; it may lead its own life. Such rigidity can even turn into soul spectres that can't be driven away. An imagination may also become arbitrary. Without roots in reality it leads to chaotic fantasy.

It is the task of the soul to keep imagination alive. This requires her to make fresh observations all the time and to activate and sharpen the physical senses she needs for this. The soul must also constantly orient herself anew in the world of ideas, and occupy herself with the development of ideas in a progressive manner.

The soul engenders experience. Experiences are conscious feelings which bring us into contact with living experiential qualities. Living experiences vibrate in the soul and make her happy. Feelings can also become rigid. Then we always experience the same thing and are always looking for that. We avoid surprise and look for confirmation. Feelings may also be chaotic and out of control. They take us for a ride. We hardly arrive fully in any experience, because feelings keep racing around in us.

The soul engenders actions. She performs deeds that cause effects. The intentions behind our deeds need not be in harmony with the effects of our actions. We may fall into fixed habits with which we want to keep life under control. If everything has been turned into fixed habits, we lock the soul up in them. Actions can also become arbitrary and turn into impulsive reactions to events.

The development of the soul manifests in the quality of our imaginations, experiences and actions. It expresses itself in the creations we introduce into the world, as well as in the purity of our inner world. As the soul schools herself, she becomes more and more herself.

In this schooling the soul can orient herself to three qualities which have been given to her, and which we know as truth, beauty and goodness.

Truth is the orientation for the imaginations we make. Is our imagination true? Does it correspond with the reality we encounter in the world? Our striving for true imagination is an anchor for the development of the soul.

Beauty is the orientation for our experience, the expression of the correct relationship, the right contrast, the perfect antithesis. It is an experiential quality, a deep awareness of what lives and works in the soul of the other.

Goodness is the orientation for our action. We can see whether we are doing the right thing from the effect our action has on the other. Does our action contribute to the developmental step the other wishes to undertake?

Question for inner reflection

The soul is not only process but also result. She appears as my imagination, my experience, my action. The qualities of imagination, experience and action reflect the state of the soul.

> *What is the situation with your imagination, experiences and actions? Are they fixed imaginations, identical experiences, routine actions? Do they develop, does the quality increase, do you make an effort, do you school yourself?*

Example

After working in organisational development for forty years I might expect that by now I know it all, I have seen it all. Not so. I see that the reality I encounter surprises and clashes with my picture of things. My experience is time and again more intense and profound than previously. In my actions I do the same things a little differently all the time. As soon as things become routine, as soon as I communicate unsurprising imaginations I already know, and do things in an established pattern, the client goes elsewhere. He notices immediately whether I am open or not.

14 IMAGE – JUDGEMENT – DECISION

Souls develop in the horizontal space they create between each other. You could say that it is intrinsic to the soul to require the 'in-between', the confluence between two. She develops between body and spirit, between 'I' and 'you', between her and him. A 'we' can then grow, a 'we-soul' that grows above and beyond the personal soul. This 'we-soul' manifests in the joint picture we build up together. Images form between us. They can develop into imaginations that enable us to behold what is essential.

The 'we-soul' also shows up in the judgements we arrive at together. Such judgement is built in a mutual process of adopting positions and discussing these. In such a we-judgment, we can see joint, supra-personal insight combined with a united direction of will.

The 'we-soul' can also be recognised in the decisions we make together. Together we move in a particular direction, we take a step together.

In our organised, self-created lives we are all the time collaborating with others in order to arrive at joint images, judgements and decisions. This is a process that constantly repeats itself and does not follow a logical course. Again and again we go through this process together: forming images, forming judgements and forming decisions. We may succeed in this if we are able to commit our own 'I' in this context and can direct this 'I' to the 'I' of the other. Success in this process depends on a more profound encounter of collaborating individuals.

Here we are confronted by external constraints that are always present: pressure of the utilitarian, demands imposed on the process by vertically structured systems of rules, regulations and procedures. We have to respond to these and allow them to orient us. That creates stress. The encounter is pushed aside, we drop each other or leave each other in the lurch if things get too difficult.

Our soul is organised in a way that enables us to handle this tension between the vertically constructed compulsion of the system and the horizontal creative space. In our childhood we were confronted by this tension when we had to navigate between freely playing games and sitting in the classroom.

The soul can stand up in both spaces. She can occupy the vertical space and make it personal, while she can open the horizontal space and make it common ground. Then image, judgement and decision can be formed as 'we-soul'.

Question for inner reflection

Souls can unite with each other. A 'we-soul' can grow. We create an image together: we share a judgement, and make a decision together. Others force us into compelling system restraints within which we have to work. Our soul adapts to the vertical. Between us we can create a horizontal space in which we give form to our images, judgements and decisions.

> *How do you collaborate with others? How are images, judgements and decisions formed? Do you experience a 'we-soul' in this?*

Example

In a meeting, the agenda is covered point by point. The chairman keeps a tight hold on procedure. Items are explained and discussed; the result is summarised and recorded. In a subsequent meeting the same items come up again - the same thing all over again.

Then, by accident, through some awkward manoeuvre by one of the participants, a real conversation gets going. Participants express themselves in a more personal manner. The chairman is surprised and gives them space. It appears that a decision taken before was not felt by the participants to be a decision. They had different views of it and evaluated the situation in different ways. After this discussion the chairman remarks that he thinks it would be a good thing if they would speak with each other like that more often.

The Soul Overcomes her Barriers and Creates her Future

The following seven triads describe expressions of the soul we need to learn to work with. The soul does not develop in a smooth, unproblematic process, but encounters much turbulence and confrontation. Our self-development is not presented to us on a silver platter: we are subjected to tests and trials. If the soul survives these, she develops into a substance-creating organ that nourishes the 'I'. The human 'I' absorbs the fruits of the soul and thereby acquires a lasting existence in the world where it originated.

15   TAKING – GIVING – SHARING

The soul needs to be autonomous, humanly creative. To achieve this she absorbs outside influences into herself. She gladly receives and takes in what she longs for.

The young soul constantly meets new impressions and has new experiences. In puberty, the soul begins to oppose or confront her environment, seeking to discover and establish her own space. The mature soul organises her own life and creates her own living and working environment. In reflecting on her life, she discovers life motifs and themes that run through it. She can then handle these more consciously. The old soul detaches herself from life and prepares to leave it.

During the course of her life the soul gladly accepts the formative influences of her environment, is open to these. The open soul also sustains injuries and is faced by unpleasant things. Initially the soul does not know how to handle this without closing herself off.

In the course of her life the soul also gradually learns to give. She wakes up to other souls around her and to their longings and needs. The soul gives to other souls out of the riches she has acquired. But the soul may be disappointed in this when her gifts are not accepted or are misused. This can likewise cause the soul to close herself off.

In living together souls learn to share. You begin to mean something for each other. For instance, you share bitter and sweet experiences, possessions, children, or ideals and ideas.

The soul can train herself to create a proper balance between this giving, receiving and sharing. One could say that she finds the golden mean and brings all three into a state of healthy balance.

Taking can be cultivated by the soul into ennobling the things taken in. She receives in gratefulness what other souls make available to her. The soul can process and enrich what she receives. In the soul, transubstantiation takes place of what comes into her. She creates new substance from what was given to her and absorbed by her, and she then hands this on to other souls who are waiting for it and need it.

Giving can be cultivated by the soul when the gift is well considered and freely offered. For a gift to be well considered the soul has to engage in real contact with the other, and make the gift in such a way that the other can also accept it in freedom. Since the effect of the acceptance reflects back to the giving soul, she in turn receives meaning from what is thereby accomplished.

Sharing can be cultivated by the soul without burdening others with things they are not at a stage to really handle, but by sharing with them what both of them can process. That creates a joint value that becomes part of their further life together.

In this sense the soul is a being in dialogue. In the interplay of taking, giving and sharing she creates values in a balanced relationship with all the other souls she encounters.

Question for inner reflection

The soul gladly receives; she also gives from her treasures. Together we share. We can cultivate taking, giving and sharing by doing this consciously and with well-considered purpose relative to the other.

How do you take, how do you give, how do you share with another? Do you feel that these three are in a healthy balance with each other? How do you ennoble your sharing, giving and receiving?

Example

In my life I have met special people who gave me their help, support and advice. They have had a decisive influence on the steps I took in my development. There are also people, young people, whom I have helped to take a new step. That gives deep satisfaction if the other then thrives. 'If you are doing well, I am also doing well.'

When I make room for the other and don't always pursue my own interests, what we jointly accomplish will be that much better. We share the result together and rejoice. This is something I have been able to observe time and again in the organisations in which I have worked and in the communities where I have lived.

16 KEEPING ONE'S WORD – ENCOUNTERING – PERFORMING A DEED

People meet each other and do things together. They may work together, go on a trip together or live together. People then become to a certain extent dependent on each other. That is a real challenge for the soul. The soul is aware of the fact that she cannot do things alone, that she is dependent on the other soul. But it is also scary for the soul to be dependent on another.

Souls make agreements with each other and need to uphold such agreements. It may happen that one person does not live up to an agreement, and then the other is disappointed. It is important for people to keep their word once it is given. Something that was started can then be better finished. When an agreement is kept it creates a deeper soul connection. You can depend on each other. When one person is fully dependent on another, for instance because of a certain handicap, then it is tricky not to let this grow into a forced dependence, but instead make a free, inner decision to enter into an obligation.

This becomes more possible if the two really meet as souls. In the encounter, the two souls make themselves known to each other. A flow can grow between souls. This can express itself in mutual fascination, possibly also in passion, in mutual longing or striving. The word 'encounter' itself already conceals a quality of relationship that is based on freedom. The soul develops inner strength in the encounter. She gets to stand on her own and find her own resources. With the encounter a conversation starts: a mutual exploration and common inspiration arise. Souls encounter other souls and go on their way together.

The encounter between souls becomes really important if deeds are performed together. Through a deed we intervene in reality and impose our will on it. By performing joint deeds, souls become attached to each other. For instance, you visit a client together, and a good advisory process then develops. That is an experience you share for years to come.

A deed works on other souls; they experience its effect. This can be favourable or unfavourable. Deeds may be accepted by others, but they may also be avoided or opposed. Actions like this also cause human soul entanglements. When souls get entangled with each other the encounter is obscured, and living up to a given promise becomes more difficult. Avoidance may develop, or conflict. In order to resolve the entanglement it can become necessary for the soul to direct her attention to someone else who can potentially bring the soul to herself again in a process of therapy.

Question for inner reflection

When people join together to do something, they give their word to each other. Keeping one's word is easier when they have had a real encounter that creates a connection. By performing a deed together that connection will grow closer. It can also lead to entanglement and conflict.

> *How do you join with others? Can you describe good examples of profound encounters? What experience did you and the other have when you performed a deed together? Are you familiar with the kind of entanglement I have described above?*

Example

With every client you take on you make agreements. These are practical agreements as to dates of meetings or delivery of services, but also strategic agreements as to the way you will work together and what results you are aiming for. You regularly evaluate together how things are going, what has been accomplished and what has failed. Then comes the moment when you go on together, make the next step together, or you can also jointly decide to end the working relationship. .

Meeting the client, doing interesting things together, can lead to a lifelong friendship. Together you have brought something into being that connects you with each other.

17 HAPPINESS – RESIGNATION – SORROW

The soul is in pursuit of happiness. Happiness is a state of soul being in which everything is in the right mutual measure or proportion, especially within our own feeling life. Happiness can be a very temporary state of soul being, but it can also be developed into a more permanent state of being.

Lasting happiness is a state in which you are close to yourself, know yourself well, without being over-preoccupied with yourself; when you are able to accept the wonder, the surprise, the setback, and give them meaning in your life. Don't we all know the feeling of intense happiness when everything comes together, the feeling of being uplifted? And also the feeling of disappointment when someone roughly interferes or intervenes and creates disorder?

The soul can embark on a path of schooling to develop strength to face setbacks. This schooling is based on the practice that the soul views everything she meets on her path – reality in the way it presents itself – as her teacher. The reality which the soul meets is wiser than the thoughts she may have about how life ought to be. With this fundamental approach, the soul can process what she has experienced and imbue it with her own meaning. When the soul feels in harmony with the life she is experiencing, she can feel herself to be in a state of happiness.

In order to hold on to this state of happiness an element of inner resignation is needed. Resignation in the soul is not the same as passivity or aloofness. Resignation is a soul state in which something new can come into being in the soul and grow to maturity. It is strengthened by expectant waiting, which is a state of equilibrium in the soul in which longing, which is future-oriented, is balanced by what is asked of the soul and approaches her as reality. When the soul is confronted by a reality that is not in alignment with what she expects, resignation can allow this misalignment to exist until the soul has integrated it. We have the tendency to place unexpected events quickly into a known frame of reference: 'O yes, I know that, I have heard that, I have seen that somewhere.' When we succeed in letting the experience stand there in our soul and look at it from different angles, after a while we give it the chance to speak for itself in us.

This may mean that the soul has to allow sorrow to be felt. The soul may come into a state in which she feels abandoned, in which she may feel offended or injured. The soul gets into a state of sorrow when, in a certain sense, she has fallen out of reality and is thrown back upon herself.

There is a fine line between happiness and sorrow. Certainly, when the soul is young her state of being can rapidly change from happiness to sorrow and back again. Later in life we can enter into these states with greater consciousness. As we age, a process of purification can take place in the soul. The soul can bear to be in a state that is not harmonious for a longer time, something she becomes capable of since our life circumstances become more fixed as we grow older. The soul may have had to let go of loved ones, or may have had to accept failures, and she entered into a condition in which she can increasingly accept or resign herself to reality.

Question for inner reflection

The human soul knows a state of happiness but also of sorrow. Resignation, which means being able to bear it and stay with it, deepens happiness and sorrow into a meaningful experience of reality.

> *How do you process happiness, how do you handle sorrow? Do you have eloquent examples of this in your life? Are you familiar with the effect of resignation in the way you deal with happiness and sorrow?*

Example

You have been very happy with a new order that has come your way. You go and meet the client, and you have a feeling that it will work well. You start the work, and after some time you notice that there are ever more obstacles. There simply is no progress. You are irritated, and when the whole thing runs aground you feel deep disappointment. You start doubting yourself.

Let things settle down, you tell yourself. You reflect on what has happened, at what point it went awry and why. You may not find a definitive answer, but in time you develop a better relationship to it. Don't rationalise it away, don't judge it, but let it stand in your soul and let it speak. That strengthens the soul.

18 OBJECTS – RELATIONSHIP – COMMUNITY

In its development, humanity has taken a path that comes closer and closer to the earth and is more and more removed from heaven. From an originally cosmic and natural existence we now live lives principally in our own material creations. We are surrounded by objects, tools and buildings which we use to give form to our life. The soul is now rooted in cars, computers, houses, offices and all kinds of 'stuff'. The objects, as we make them, are lifeless in themselves. They have purpose only if the soul gives purpose to them. The soul has made herself at home in a world of objects and can utilise these for her own processes. What especially occupies the soul today is technical communication and all its various devices. GPS, the internet and email enable the soul to move with incredible speed through the world without having to come into direct contact with other souls. Human souls can live in virtual worlds. This may lead to a situation where the soul avoids direct contact with others, the living encounter. The soul learns to live indirectly and thus creates the space for herself in which she is free to accept or reject anything she pleases.

In direct contact the soul is confronted with the other soul, and is forced to establish some kind of relationship. Human souls who live together for a lifetime may grow together and in a sense become one soul. Relationship is what the human soul seeks. In direct economic transactions, too, the soul comes into contact with others. There also, the relationship and how it should be nourished is the element which we value as important. The relationship becomes personal and intimate when we address the other person by name. Our name is an expression of the soul we are. To be addressed by the other by your name opens the door to intimate contact.

The human soul co-exists with other souls in communities formed by human beings. These may be natural communities such as family or nation, but may also be organised communities such as a business or a club. In such communities souls can find each other and enter into relationships. This is expressed in the words:

The healthy social life is found when in the mirror of each human soul the whole community finds its reflection, and when in the community the virtue of each one is living.

Souls strive for growth and development. This can take place in communities in which the soul lives and works. In my relationship with the other, what the other has built up can become mine, and vice versa. We enter into a process of dialogue with each other in which the soul can unfold so that the individuality itself comes in to its own, develops its own unique qualities in the encounter.

Question for inner reflection

We have surrounded ourselves with objects. We are clothed in a material world with which we deal every day. Distance develops between human beings; we can ignore each other. We no longer live as a matter of course in our own natural communities. But it is a good thing when we ourselves create a community of people from which we draw the strength for further steps in our development.

> *What communities are you part of? How do they enhance your life? How do you handle all the 'stuff' you have around you? Does your soul seek relationships with others?*

Example

Almost every day, and increasingly so, I am busy responding to emails and sending my own emails to others. I look for information on the internet, buy things there, book trips, sign up for things. On Facebook and Linked-in, two network sites, I am invited daily to connect with others. Thus I have an extremely widespread network of contacts with other people; however, I hardly ever physically meet them. This is in stark contrast with my beloved family and a few friendships which have nourished my soul for many years with shared life experiences. For me, the work communities in which I have for many years experienced fascinating processes of development together with colleagues are the ones that strongly call on the strength of my 'I'. Here I find my companions in spirit and destiny.

19 HATE – GUILT – FEAR

The soul is a paradox and strives for harmony. But something completely different may also happen. The soul may be so disturbed by someone else that hate rises up in her. Such hate announces itself when the soul – at great cost – wants to invalidate or crush another soul. Hate may arise because the other does not fit into my world iew, or has done me an injustice, is continually in my way, or especially if he threatens me. Hate can lead to actions or inner curses aimed at thwarting the other. A person who was once loved may, as time passes, become hated. The process by which this occurs is a stealthy, insidious one. The soul gradually becomes ever more possessed of dark images of the other soul, which haunt her. In time these images harden the soul – the other soul turns into a spectre, and spectres must be fought.

Parallel with this the soul develops feelings of guilt. Conscience presents itself, and a voice whispers that this is not OK. The voice is silenced; the soul refuses to hear it. At unexpected moments feelings of guilt rise up more strongly. They torment the soul and are forcefully suppressed. The soul rationalises her hate-filled stance.

All this conceals a continual experience of fear. The soul feels unsafe and assaulted by the other soul. Fear is like a fog that comes down into the soul and prevents her from seeing clearly. There is a continual risk of collision, of being attacked. This fear feeds the hate vis-à-vis the threatening soul.

Where does fear come from? Initially, already, with our mother's milk: a fear of annihilation. Fear can be fostered by parents who want to protect their child from (supposed) threats. When we experience some kind of failure or blow of fate, we become afraid that this will be repeated. Fear lodges itself in the soul and is hard to dislodge. Dealing with fear is a tall order for every soul. In the end, we must look fear in the eye. We begin by voicing it, by sharing our feelings of fear with others. Consciousness of fear becomes stronger if you can stay with the feelings without running away from them. In that situation a sun, a light, can break through the fog and assuage the shadow. The shadow becomes visible in a way that we can cope with. Voicing guilt feelings and sharing them can shine a light on the spectre of hate.

Question for inner reflection

The soul can be possessed by fear. Fear pervades us, paralyses us. In a soul full of fear, hate has free play. 'I do not want the other; he has to disappear out of my life.' Hate impels me to irresponsible behaviour. When I come to myself again I feel guilt. 'I shouldn't have done that.' Fear, hate and guilt create uncontrollable forces in the soul. My 'I' is too weak to put the brakes on those forces. The other will have to help me overcome them.

> *Are you familiar with such fear in the soul? How do you deal with this subtle hate that wishes to put the other out of action or thwart him? How do you handle guilt feelings? Do you have examples?*

Example

The colleague with whom I share ultimate responsibility for our venture unexpectedly accuses me of abusing my position. At first, he drops suggestive hints about me favouring certain individuals. Later the allegations become more direct. Am I financially trustworthy? What about those invoices? After a while it keeps me awake at night. I am finding this colleague, whom I used to like so much, a miserable problem that requires strong action. But that isn't working, and I feel weakened. Every reply I give him is evaded and rejected as proof of untrustworthiness. It is turning into a conflict.

It is going to be either you or me. In the end he leaves. An occurrence like that keeps rumbling in the soul for years. What was it? How did I do that? Why? And why in this way?

20   DISTANCING – AVERSION – RESISTANCE

The soul likes to be involved with what is going on around her. She is curious and wants to find out about things. But the soul can also equally withdraw and distance herself. That happens when things come too close so that the soul becomes caught in her own reflections, her own involvement. She feels oppressed and wants to free herself. She can do that by withdrawing into her own secure being. Other souls may try to prevent her from doing this. They hold on to the soul and do not want to let go of her. Then the soul can feel compelled even more strongly to withdraw and, by withdrawing, to become stuck in self-defence.

Such distancing becomes stronger the more aversion is felt. Perhaps this happens because the soul makes aesthetic objections to something, she has different tastes and does not feel comfortable. It can also be a stronger experience: the soul feels assaulted, or even abused or enslaved. The soul longs for purity and respect. She wants to be treated with consideration by the other.

The soul may not just feel aversion, she may also show great resistance. The soul puts up a fight and wants to defeat the other, thus entering into conflict.

Distancing oneself from the other, feelings of aversion to the other, resistance against the other can escalate in a relationship. It is precisely in situations where two souls are closely involved with each other, but enter into conflict with each other, that such escalation can occur. Initially there are only small irritations that can be quickly overcome through positive feelings and self-criticism. However, irritation can cross a boundary if its source becomes stronger. The soul becomes fixated, she narrows her view, armours herself and reacts more aggressively. By getting progressively more excited or, remarkably, the opposite, cooling off, the soul reaches the next threshold: the thought of dismissing or condemning the other. The other is denigrated, made into a spectacle, pushed aside and attacked. Shrewd tactics can serve here that may end in a kind of guerrilla warfare.

Such mutual conflict can degenerate into a fight to the death. This has a powerful effect on the inner life of the soul. She is eaten up by venom, chilled by aversion, and weakened by a lack of love, respect and creative space. The soul is even capable of causing her own demise in this way: she can perish and die.

Souls can allow themselves to be saved by other souls who, oriented toward the health of this particular soul, can see the drama unfold. Here we see the significance of friendship. Faithful friends can accompany the soul on her path. Friendship opens the way for a glimpse into the inner world of the other and, vice versa, for a glimpse by the other into one's own inner world. Friends support one another in difficult moments. And it is in the drama of life that we come to know our real friends. Friends see the difference between who you are and what has developed in you. They can unravel knots in the soul and can assist you in finding the next step forward.

Question for inner reflection

There are moments or periods in life when things are not going well for the soul. She withdraws, distances herself. She is filled with aversion and mounts resistance. The soul is embarking on destructive behaviour. The end may be self-destruction.

> *Are you familiar with these destructive forces in yourself? How do they determine your soul, and what do you do to counteract them?*

Example

In our relationship with our life partner there are times when things do not go smoothly. Very subtly the soul distances herself from the other. You see more and more weaknesses in the other, the shadow, the incapacity. At certain moments this calls forth aversion; you don't feel good with the other. Situations and arrangements happen that awaken resistance in the soul. 'I am not going to do that.'

A conflict is growing between the partners that can escalate. In the end a separation may be the only way out. Does it ever come right again? Old wounds are easily ripped open.

21 CONFIRMATION – MOVEMENT – CHANGE

The soul who is being oppressed can be rescued by other souls, when the 'I' that lives in her is addressed. This 'I' takes possession of the soul when called on by another 'I'. Because the 'I' is recognised and addressed in the soul, the latter can feel inner confirmation in her deepest essence, the foundation of her existence. That is true friendship.

The soul is brought into movement by the other if she allows herself to be questioned. The fact of asking the other the 'I' question forms the beginning of a process of soul healing.

This may begin with the question: 'What is happening?' Then comes the question: 'What is going on with you? How can I help you so that you can take a step forward?' An encounter of two 'I's is taking place here. They bring each other into movement.

Every soul has an open wound she would like to heal. By being addressed and brought into movement the soul can be liberated from her oppression. Then souls move forward and explore new territory together.

In this process of change, the soul can transform herself to a higher level of consciousness, 'I' consciousness. Born from hereditary sources and formed in dialogue with her surroundings, the soul can, in union with the 'I', develop into a conscious soul who embraces her 'karma' or destiny. This means that the individualised soul becomes connected with 'brothers and sisters in spirit'. These are the 'I's of other souls who open themselves to a similar ideal. These souls enter into a free, spiritual dialogue with each other, which helps every individual soul develop higher consciousness.

The soul transforms hereditary substance – which is anchored in our genes – into her own spiritual assets. She develops capacities of a higher order than the talents with which she came into the world. The soul also transforms the way she was schooled and formed by her educators and teachers. She makes the lessons her own, and transforms them into higher insights.

The soul also transforms her own unique constellation, the individual personality. She becomes an authentic soul with whom other souls can identify. She turns into a creative soul capable of showing the world the right thing, inspiring truth, bringing experience of the beautiful, doing the good. The soul becomes a blessing for others and a source of inspiration for her own 'I'.

The substance of the soul is absorbed in this, her own 'I'. The 'I' clothes itself in this substance, and can carry this substance across the threshold of death. There the soul will undergo her own reflective catharsis, the encounter with her past life. She will be able to transform herself into a living 'I' spirit.

Question for inner reflection

The soul goes through painful processes, but through these she is able to transform herself towards a higher state of consciousness. She becomes more conscious of herself, but also of the social dynamic in which she is dwelling. The appeal from my 'I' to the 'I' of the other leads to confirmation: 'I am' and 'It is right that I am here in this set of circumstances.' This being an 'I' is a state of constant change and constant movement. In this way the 'I' of the human being is nourished by soul substance – which forms itself in change and movement – towards a higher state of being.

> *How do you describe the transformations you undergo, the changes that are taking place in you? Through what movements do they become possible? How does your authentic 'I' make itself visible here?*

Example

For many years now I have investigated how leadership functions in organisations. From discussions with many people in leadership positions, what stands out is that only a leader's self-acquired insight really works effectively on other people. Working with personally acquired insight works right through into the encounter with the other. The other then becomes able to take a step forward; together we make progress. It is the authentic personality that makes the difference. We arrive in a state of soul being that enables us to make the impulse we are working with fruitful in the interaction with the clients we are serving.

Conclusion of Part 1

I have described the language of the soul in twenty-one triads. This reflects an effort to bring the language of the soul into the organised life we lead. When in the organised context of our lives we become more conscious of our own soul life and that of others, the possibility arises to achieve a form of community worthy of human beings. It is possible likewise for the soul to embark on conscious development, also within our organised context.

In this way the soul passes through three developmental stages. In the first stage the soul is all feeling and sensation. She experiences what happens around her, engaging with events. She observes and she builds experience in these feelings. The soul becomes conscious of herself when the human 'I', the spiritual core, takes up its dwelling in the soul. The 'I' will do so when it senses the appeal of another person.

When the soul becomes conscious of her feelings, she can begin to take the reality she has observed in hand and start working on it. The soul now forms clear thoughts, she achieves more conscious experiences and becomes able to transform her feelings and sensations into conscious deeds. The soul creates for herself an inner structure in which she can exist.

She lives with images, known emotions; she recognises what is going on. In this way the soul builds her intelligence and her sensitivity, and she develops intuitive feeling in her actions.

When the soul is subsequently confronted by complexities with which she is unfamiliar, encountering the unknown in foreign territory, her own 'I' can wake her up so that, using the capacities of this 'I', she learns to deal with such complexities. She will not want to control these, or distance herself from them, but will want to develop her consciousness through these complexities. What develops then is an 'I' soul in open dialogue, moving, searching and reflecting from situation to situation in the effort to penetrate to the essence of what arises. The soul becomes a seer. She develops her triads into sense organs for the life she encounters. She is increasingly able to acquire a conscious relationship with the complexities of reality, and to handle these in a creative, fruitful manner.

To transform themselves into conscious 'I' souls, human beings need to embark of a path of schooling. This will be the subject of part 2.

PART 2

THE SCHOOLING OF THE SOUL

Introduction

Throughout my life I have worked with the question of how I can develop consciousness in the social realm with others. What is taking place, what is playing itself out, how do I and the other deal with that? How do I learn to recognise the effect I have on the other, how do I know what is the right thing to do? How do I take responsibility while yet leaving the other free? More than anything else it has been the practical life I lead that has shown me the way here. I would like to outline a few examples.

As a teenager I was struck by the experience that coping with rough kids in a clubhouse in the centre of town, and at the same time practising meditation in a monastery, both helped me find my centre. These experiences gave me a strong connection with truly practical social questions, as well as with my inner longing also to connect with these questions reflectively and in a creative, responsible way.

As a sociology student I explored issues such as the significance of values and norms in the community. At the same time I was also 'social secretary' in the student community and as such responsible for the accommodation and social welfare of students. I began to see that the outer world of our existence needs a connection with the inner world of our ideals and strivings.

When employed by Shell Nederland I was asked to monitor organisational development processes in which staff could ask themselves questions about their work processes and the quality of their collaboration, with an eye to improving working practice. I began to see that people are living in processes, and that when they can participate in the process of development of their organisation they can connect their inner world of values and strivings with that development.

In my consulting work I accompany people and organisations on their path of development. In extensive processes I collaborate as facilitator with the leadership and community of all kinds of organisations to achieve creative and meaningful developmental steps. I can explore the space of horizontal, non-hierarchical leadership and, in shared responsibility with others, bring something new and significant into existence. At the same time I can give meaning and content to my own soul.

In this lifelong process of exploration and experiment some fundamental possibilities for personal development in the social realm have gradually revealed themselves to me. Step by step I have begun to realise that the long-term practice of working with the social question in order to give meaningful support to my clients is in effect a path of schooling for my own authentic personality. This became even more evident to me when I immersed myself in the new path of schooling, the 'Saturn Way', developed by Rudolf Steiner and Bernard Lievegoed. This path exists side by side with what they called the Moon way, which is a personal meditative path for schooling one's own soul. The Saturn path is the path of schooling we can travel when, based on a 'scientific' approach, we bring our own 'I' to consciousness in dialogue and interaction with the community, and learn to see this 'I' beyond its immediate effects in the world and surrounding environment.

This is the path of schooling I want to describe here. My aim is to present a path of schooling of the soul which anyone of good will can pursue. It helps develop an organ of perception in the social realm, together with the capacity to engage with social questions in a conscious and appropriate way, both in the organisational context in which one is involved and in one's personal life. Through this path of schooling we develop an organ of perception for forces that work among us human souls, and for the way we can stand up as spiritual beings within these forces. This has meaning for our own spiritual core as well as for humanity as a whole.

This path of schooling distinguishes itself from many others because it does not in the first place involve personal, self-oriented meditative activity, but instead connects primarily with the processes experienced by the 'I' in the community in which it participates. Such communities are not normally the natural communities of which everyone automatically forms part through birth, but they are, in particular, the organised communities which one joins by one's own decision.

The principal elements of this path of schooling are threefold:

- Relating to each other while undertaking the task of this community within the greater whole of human society
- One's own personal orientation in this community
- Shared, but also personal processing of the experiences gained in this community

Studying the text of this book can be a first step on the path of schooling described here. The various aids that are given in the text are important and can be applied to your own situation. It begins with observation and practice in your own life of soul and soul qualities described in Part 1, as the lens through which we observe the social realm. What is seen there can be connected with our own personality in order to arrive at the capacity for conscious deed.

In support of this schooling of observation and action I include practical exercises here and there that can reinforce the process. As well as enhancing our own self-development, self-chosen study and personal meditation can strengthen the significance of our observations, experiences and insights for the community of which we form a part.

Paths of Schooling

In his book on paths of schooling, Bernard Lievegoed distinguishes the Moon way and the Saturn way. He describes the Moon way as a path that has been known for a very long time as a way for the individual human being to attain insight into higher worlds. It is a meditative path pursued primarily in inner activity. The essence of this path is that the individual becomes conscious in silent attention of what is occurring in his inner world, and how this acquires significance for the deeds he performs in the outer world.

In the course of the centuries initiated masters have repeatedly developed and described paths of this nature. For instance, Buddha taught the eightfold path for developing inner qualities that can elevate our soul. We can also practise mantras or sacred texts, the frequent repetition of which can configure our inner world. Sometimes such paths are designed to overcome the disturbing inner voice of our ego, but sometimes their intention is, equally, to strengthen the individual ego and develop it to a higher level.

In addition to the Moon way, Bernard Lievegoed describes the Saturn way, a new path the human being can take as part of the community for which he feels responsible. Here the individual connects his destiny with that of the community of which he forms a part. It is a path of schooling which, in essence, represents a process of personal leadership in a community of people. It is a new path because in our time we can discern ever more strongly the development of individual consciousness, which searches for a conscious relationship to everything it encounters around itself.

In the book rererred to above, Lievegoed wrote:

There is also a different path of development, one which is completely new for human development and was not possible before our time. It is connected with the scientific approach humanity has taken since the fifteenth century. Previously, the outer world had meaning for the human being only to the extent that it was able to enrich his inner world. The first beginnings of efforts to understand the outer world on its own, separately from the human being, were undertaken by Greek philosophers. This approach to the world was not able to really break through until modern times. [...]

The human being investigates Creation for the sake of Creation itself, not for any experience in his own soul. If performed in the right manner, this form of facing the world is a lofty human deed. Gaining insight into the world is a highly creative act, something we are able to add to Creation to enhance and complement it.

The path of schooling described in this book is intended as a more practical addition to Bernard Lievegoed's description of the Saturn way. It can offer us the possibility of travelling this path with a conscious soul. The dimensions of the path described here will help a person, in interaction with others, to consciously nurture the coherence of his soul. This will enable us to have a healing effect in the organised communities in which we live. It can help me and the other to realise our own destiny.

The Basis for the Path of Schooling in the Social Realm

When we wish to pursue a path of schooling in the social realm, to develop ourselves as a spiritual being and reach a higher level of consciousness, it is important to first find a good foundation for this effort. *We can find this foundation if we are able to see and experience the social realm as a question.*

'Question' is a good expression for the reality in which we live. A question is in essence the expression of the human soul in the social reality in which she exists. This reality – I'd like to stress this – is not the same as the reality which can be characterised as divine and natural Creation, of which we are also part. We are part of a world of nature and spirit that was fashioned and is nurtured by divine creative beings. At the same time, we also form part of a world created by human beings, which lies in the hands of individual human beings and of human community. There we find the social realm, in the relationship between 'I' and community.

The remarkable thing about the human soul is that she was created as a divine potential, but can only be brought into existence and maturity through human life. Wonderful examples of this divine potential are visible in the creative work of spiritual leaders of humanity throughout the ages. For instance, we can think of the spiritual treasures of Buddha and Zarathustra, of Christian Rosenkreutz, Krishnamurti and Rudolf Steiner. They show us examples of a human soul emerging from the divine and fulfilling her destiny amidst, and in encounter with, the paradoxes of earthly existence.

The destiny of the human soul is to achieve freedom. That is the unique and ultimate human value we can create with each other in our human context, which gains significance when added to the divinely created world in which we find ourselves. We consider the story of Christ, described as a universal being, as a shining example of the way in which this human value of freedom can be attained and added to divine Creation.

The path in life which every individual human being can take truthfully and consciously within the community, if she or he decides to do that, is one I see as the basis for creating this freedom. In this light I now want to describe this social path of schooling.

LIVING WITH A QUESTION

As I have indicated, the human being lives in a context of organised communities, in which there is no natural harmony and cohesion and in which, for this reason, the laws of nature do not apply. Only principles acquired or developed by human beings work there. This humanly created world manifests in the material constructions we build, and in which we live, travel and work. This humanly created world also becomes visible in the laws, rules and customs with which we regulate our mutual interaction.

The world also comes to expression in human works of art, in acquired knowledge, in the published word. Existence in this humanly created world is not harmonious but paradoxical. It consists of polarities, of opposing forces. It is thus a world of different layers and 'dis-relationships'. For instance, what we think may not be what we do. And the world of experience in a top management function differs from that of the worker on the shop floor. People's perceptions differ; they don't share the same judgements and interpretations.

Not only do we know rich and poor, we also know natural and artificial, erudite and dull, inclusive and exclusive, interested and removed. Our world of dis-relationships expresses itself in questions that surface in and around human beings. This world, which has, in a sense, collapsed under mutually opposing forces, invites us to create new forces of cohesion to bring it together again.

The perception of problems and the discovery of dis-relationships represent the first step on the path of development of the human being and the human community.

In practical life we encounter adversity, resistance, boundaries and barriers which we have to learn to surmount. There is not much that happens all by itself. In our environment we also encounter a multitude of problems others are struggling with.

But what are the problems to which we direct our attention? How can we make the problems that matter to us our own? How can we start working on them? We can find all kinds of excuses to avoid a problem we are encountering. We can take flight into the past, or leap into the future. Problems may sometimes strike us with fear and inner repulsion. Don't we all prefer to live our lives undisturbed and carefree, both in ourselves and with each other?

The confrontation with problems leads to a second phase: we begin to live with a question.

How does a question develop? Because we meet with surprises in daily life, because our expectations meet with unexpected hindrances, because things are different from what we wish, we undergo trials and tribulations and must pay fresh attention all the time to what is happening and what has happened. Life forces us to take time off now and then to reflect on what has happened so that we may re-establish contact with the reality that is being enacted in our lives. By taking a little distance now and then from what is going on, and thinking about what is taking place in and around us, a question will arise in us. A question is really the concretisation of a process of wanting to know and have insight. The question arises in us and may sometimes grow into a permanent companion in our lives.

In my life I woke up in this way to the question of the relationship between human development and organisational development. Perhaps you would expect that after living with this question for more than forty years I would have found the answer. But the answer is still not there. However, the question has become more and more decisive for the discoveries and insights I have gained in my life.

The question works like a magnet: it attracts perceptions and experiences. By living with a question we can discover worlds we would not otherwise have seen. The question directs your perception in a sense; it helps you see things others do not see. In this way problems come to life, perceptions become possible that enable the problem to speak and give us things to reflect on, and thus we gain progressively more insight.

The question develops into questioning, the third phase.

Social reality can speak to us reflectively if we approach it in a questioning mode. We can do this by entering into conversation with people we meet and by giving their problems our attention, by asking them questions. Initially we will tend to question the other with the aim of making progress ourselves through the answers. In a certain sense we make use of the other for our own quest. This will cause us to build our own insights on the basis of what others are saying to us, in the same way as, when watching a film or reading a book, we absorb the content as nourishment for our inner world. The art of questioning, however, involves allowing our primary interest to go out to the other, and enabling the other to tell us his story in response to our questions.

Our questions help the other to tell us the story better; the story of the other comes to life in both of us. This demands a fundamental attitude in the questioner, namely that it is not his primary goal to understand what the other tells him. After all, we can only understand our own representation, our own image of what the other is telling us. The idea is to listen in such a way that our interest invites the other to elaborate more and more on the interesting details of his story. In this way, the story of the other comes to life in the other himself, and also in us.

Here we hit upon the significance of the so-called 'detour principle'. By orienting ourselves to the other it is as if we create a space in our soul in which our own questions can be nurtured.

It is an interesting fact that when the other is living with a problem, our questions can help him or her to bring the problem into development. If after some time we ask the other to put his problem into words again, the story he will then relate will lead to a reformulation of the question. This will not necessarily be a better formulation than the first one. Rather, the problem will prove to have completely different aspects, and by telling the story again, light is thrown on these new aspects. The fact that the problem is now formulated in a different way creates in the person who is living with it an opportunity to view it and deal with it in a new way. The other can take a step forward which moves the problem on.

What is happening here between me and the other can be viewed as a process of dialogue, of speaking and listening. Living with our own question and asking questions of the other together form the basis for our personal path of schooling in the social realm. When we are living with a question, all kinds of processes take place in us - involving analysis, puzzling, interpreting, suffering and reflection. In the conversation with the other, these thoughts and feelings rise up strongly. We can experience our problem anew.

As questioner we have the tendency to give all our attention to our own feelings and interpretations that arise while we are listening to the other. This shows up, for instance, in the attention we give to all kinds of things in the background, to our looking for explanations of why things happened the way they did, to our judgement of what has occurred. We have an opinion about what the other is telling us, we want to understand it completely, are eager to make immediate suggestions. It takes restraint – which can be practised - to hold back with these interpretations, judgements and suggestions, and instead pay attention to fully describing events and situations in which the problem manifests.

Because we help the other describe with precision what has happened, where and when it occurred, and who was involved, we as questioner will get a better insight ourselves into the nature of the process and narrative. The problem of the other rises up before us and takes shape.

When, in telling the story, we form images of the problem, and when, drawing on actual events and occurrences, it is told differently again and again, the problem comes to life in both the person himself and the questioner. This helps us overcome stereotype interpretations and judgements. We begin to realise that the problem is different from what we initially thought. Then an inner space can open up within us to meet the person in his process and to be of help to him in finding the next step in the process. This will enable us as questioner to help someone who is living with a question, by giving him valuable tips for action which occurred to us while we were listening. These tips for action may help the questioner arrive at an inner decision to take a new step forward that did not at first seem possible. Thus a self-chosen path opens up into the future. We grow and develop through this: our soul is moved, our spirit broadens its outlook.

When we live with a question the encounter with the other will act as a magnet to give us the nourishment we crave for the development of our soul. When, in the encounter with the other, we open ourselves to his problem, when we question the other so that he can tell us his story and find his next step forward, we will also strengthen our own individual personality as it seeks to enter on a path of schooling in the social realm.

2   We live with a question  3   We meet the other.
Through it we perceive   We question the other and his
what at first we had not seen.   problem and he takes a new step.

1   Our lives consist of problems.
We are confronted
with dis-relationships.

Exercise

In every encounter with another human being the following qualities can be nurtured:

- Perceiving the other with all senses wide open
- Opening yourself to the other's question
- Entering into the other's question by sharing with him what moves you in your own search
- Supporting the other when he takes a feasible step forward
- Making conscious how this encounter contributes to the way you live with your own question

PITFALLS
- Measuring the other by your own judgements;
- Forcing your own ideas on the other
- Judging what the other relates by what you know already, and fitting this into the framework of thoughts and feelings you already feel comfortable with
- Wanting to offer solutions that work for you, but are possibly not feasible for the other
- Using the other for the satisfaction of your own longings
- Moralising by imposing psychological demands on the behaviour of the other
- Interpreting what happened as confirmation of what you yourself consider important and valuable

Living with a question oneself, and questioning the other, so that consciousness for the problem grows and new steps forward can be discovered – these together form the foundation for the following three basic qualities of the personal path of schooling in the practical social realm: living in a process, living in dialogue, and living fully within one's own biography.

LIVING IN A PROCESS

Life takes its course in us. It is a process that enacts itself in us from birth to death. In this life process we gain all our experiences and observations, and bring meaning to them. We are formed by the genetic inheritance we have received from our parents and ancestors, by all our encounters and experiences, and by the environment in which we work and which works on us. We are formed by our own impulses that well up out of our unique personality and lead us to actions. In this way we develop into a multi-faceted personality that reveals itself to others through the course of our life.

We form a body, which we nourish and take care of; this body becomes our dwelling place. It is the wonderful cosmic and hereditary gift which carries us through time. We are also given a span of time in which to live and in which the course of our life is enacted. The course of life has periods in which our soul and our being can develop in a cyclical way. We are born and live as baby and child, we experience puberty, grow into adulthood, we set off into the world and construct our life, we go through crises, grow older and have to let go and die. Along the way, however, this curve of life may be rudely interrupted by things that happen to us.

In this biographical trajectory we engage in life processes. We feed ourselves, take care of our body, learn and study, work and consume. We build our dwelling place, create our organisation, sleep, rest and take vacations; and we reflect. All of this takes place between past and future, in the present. Life happens to us, and we also create it ourselves; it has ups and downs, but also its own inevitable continuity.

While initially we simply undergo this life and have to surrender to it, as time goes on the potential increases for us to see our life as a totality of processes that occur cyclically, and which we can learn to nurture consciously and actively. We make this discovery by becoming conscious of the fact that life is a cycle of events that continually, rhythmically recur. There are natural rhythms of life, such as waking and sleeping, eating and washing, action and reflection, meeting and withdrawing, breathing in and out, taking in and giving away.

Now, it is an art in life to learn to view consciously the processes in which we live – how they are enacted, how they address us cyclically, and how these rhythms can be observed and cultivated. This opens the way for us to integrate processes and rhythms into our life by our own will and intent, alongside the natural processes and rhythms in which we live.

I will give some examples.

- It is possible to undertake a review of the day every evening before going to sleep. What took place today, whom did I meet, when was I attentive and when wasn't I, what surprised me? By doing this regularly, in a daily rhythm – by becoming a spectator of ourselves, you might say – the capacity develops in us to go through life with a certain wakefulness or attentiveness.

- Each morning, while getting ready for the day, we can take care of our body using healing or essential oils. Thus we briefly pay attention to how the body is feeling, how our skin breathes.

- When we eat we can be more conscious of the way we take in our nourishment. Not only can we make more conscious choices as to what we eat and how much, but the act of eating itself can be formed into a conscious, rhythmic process that supports the digestion of the food we eat.

- Once a year we can go to the doctor and have a check-up to assess the health of our organs.

In ways like this our life can be supported by all kinds of self-chosen rituals with the aim of giving attention to what we consider important.

But I can also give conscious attention to others. Children can, before they go to sleep, listen to a story that you read to them with full interest and attention. Festival days with a religious background can become more meaningful when we stop and think about stories which give us increased insight into our own lives.

When we see life as a totality of processes, and when we nurture these, we can help ourselves develop conscious awareness of the forces at work in these processes. The processes of sleeping, eating, working, exercising, being together, learning, caring and so on, each develop their own significance in time. As a result of our conscious intervention we build up our own substance in these processes. Thus we begin to deepen our life within them. Over and above the routine nature of our life, our consciousness is growing and developing. In this way every process can be connected, according to its own nature, with cosmic and earthly sources. We enter into a connection with what the earth bestows on us and, at the same time, we are connected with cosmic nourishment.

Out of this we can develop an art of life that accepts each process for its intrinsic value, rather than confusing things by seeking to bring into one process what belongs in another. For instance, we may find that the process of dining late interferes with the process of sleeping. Or we may discover that our work process continues during our time with our loved ones at home. Or we may see that what occurs in the process of our marriage or relationship works through into the way we work – or don't - on our personal development. We can easily get confused when our life processes get mixed up with each other. It is an art in life to give each process its dues, to nurture it with the attention it needs, and to place and keep the processes in proper relationships with each other.

By becoming conscious of which processes we are living in at any time, and by discovering the particular character of each process and deepening it, we can attain a higher quality of life. As multi-faceted beings we can take responsibility for these processes: they can enable us to guide and govern our life energy.

We are not alone in these processes. All the time we meet others who also live in such processes. Human encounters enable us to strengthen each other in our processes; however, we can also weaken each other by getting in each other's way. By allowing the other to have what is his or hers, and by being in contact with what is our own, we can create healthy conditions in social dynamics. When we get mixed up in each other's processes and can no longer distinguish what belongs to whom, we get ensnared in life and lose sight of our potential development. We can help the other and ourselves to stay out of such senseless complications by adopting clear positions in the processes in which we live.

As a father bringing up his child, I can arrive at the insight that it is my child who is educating me, and that it is my task to be clear as to where boundaries lie of what is allowed or not. Or, as a manager I can take the position that every member of staff should not just do his work in a responsible way, but should also take responsibility for improving his own work process when the customer requires this.

Taking a position becomes possible when we are in touch with our own interests and also respect the interests of the other. Self-interest does not have to be an egotistic, self-serving endeavour, for which we exploit the other, but should be a state of awareness of what is important for oneself, of one's own position and striving, while bringing this into relationship with what is important for the other. This enables us and the other to see where we mutually stand so we can create clear, fruitful interaction and collaboration between us.

Exercise

As a first step you can examine your own life to see which processes are occurring for you. You can do this by tracing which activities repeat themselves cyclically on a regular basis. Think, for instance, of work activities, family activities, personal learning activities and so on. Give a name to each of these various cycles of activity.

As a second step, take a close look at each of these cycles of activity, and ask yourself whether a process is in healthy flow or whether it stagnates repeatedly and causes annoyance or conflict. By examining the rhythm in encounters with others who are involved in the process, by looking at the predominant themes and recurring phenomena, you may find the right point of intervention in the process that may lead to a good flow.

As a third step you may try to cultivate or develop the process. In order to prevent the process from becoming routine and getting into a rut, you can always look for small variations in your own behaviour which can preserve originality or spontaneity, also for the other people involved in the process.

The purpose of these steps is to gain clarity and to arrive at a certain soul hygiene in life. In this regard it is a good exercise to keep what is taking place in one process separate from what is happening in others. We have the tendency to bother each other with our own emotions and reactions which, however, the other cannot feel in the same way because they do not form part of the world of joint experience. This is not to say that we cannot share thoughts and feelings with each other. But we should not burden someone with expectations that he or she should do something about our thoughts and feelings.

PITFALLS
- The idea that something like this is not possible for me because I experience my life as too hectic and unpredictable
- Others are the cause of what happens in my life - I have no control over it
- I want to have full control over my life and I arrange things in such a way that there can be no surprises
- I have no time for such questions; tomorrow I will have forgotten my good intentions anyway
- It does not matter so much what I do and how I do it – this does not affect my own feelings and thoughts
- I share my feelings and thoughts with everyone I meet.

Points of view for realising a process

The realisation and organisation of our life processes is an art we can gradually learn. The following points of view will help with this.

- At the basis of every process is a problem that lives in us. I have described a problem as a dis-relationship which wants to be transformed into a healthy relationship. For instance, I may be living with the problem of getting enough sleep, or the problem of making a meaningful contribution to my work, or that of earning sufficient income to support for my family. Becoming more conscious of what the problem is that feeds and gives meaning to the process, enables me to be more present in the process as it is taking place.
- Becoming conscious of the desired result of a process, and whether this result is actually being achieved. I sleep with the purpose of being rested the next day; am I indeed rested or was my sleep disturbed, and do I have to look for ways to get that right? Is the goal of my work to establish a career, and is that actually happening? Is my family life close and cosy or are there a lot of quarrels? Is the collaboration with my colleagues creative and inspiring? If we have a clear picture in mind of what our goal is we can be more alert to what is actually happening, and whether this is in accord with what we would like to see and experience.
- The premise which we want as the basis for managing the process, along with the question of which premises actually govern it. Are the desired and actual conceptions aligned with each other? I would like to have a restful vacation; however, after the vacation I am tired because of all the efforts I made to entertain myself. I want interesting work which helps me develop, but I am overcome by the stress of the work and by my ambition to be in complete control of everything. I want to give the family my attention, but I don't have enough time and my contact with them ends up being perfunctory and hurried. I would very much like to enjoy things, but am always annoyed at other people. Becoming conscious of our attitudes, and of the effects they have in an actual social dynamic, opens the door for us to wake up to new ideas. Making a new idea your own means that you are laying the foundation for a different way of acting.
- The way we deal with time. Am I living in a rhythm in which I can be really present? Am I too late, am I in a place where I really do not want to be, am I caught in all kinds of necessities that keep me from being where I want to be and doing what I experience as meaningful? It is good practice always to be a little ahead of things, to be inwardly prepared, to be present

a little early so that you can really arrive. It is helpful to be present in the situation, and to do what you were asked to do, and what you experience as meaningful. Processes compete with each other for time, pushing each other out of the way and demanding attention. Can I find the right rhythm, and be there at the right moment?

- Mobilization of the means [not clear what 'means' means! Please define...] I need for my process. If I am capable of generating these means, then they will be appropriate and effective. Am I caught up in all the material aspects, and have the means therefore become the end? Or have the means been consciously chosen so that they serve the process? Too much can be just as much a burden as too little.
- Discovering core meaning in our own life. Is there a theme in our life that always accompanies us, and that gives meaning to what is occupying us? The discovery of our own core theme creates a fundamental principle of order in all the choices we make. We can discover this theme as we go through life by asking, 'What is it that wakes me up, that brings me to life and enthusiasm and gives me a deeper feeling of meaning?'

In the lives and works of great artists such as Rembrandt or Van Gogh we can see how a human being can passionately work all his life to bring his own inmost theme to expression. But we may also perceive, say, how a physician hearkens to his desire to heal; or how a teacher commits himself every day of his life to teach young children a foreign language and culture.

When we sleep through life, when we are disengaged, then the connection with our own theme, our own life question, is broken. Our own theme nourishes the passionate fulfilment of our life: it is our most important wellspring, and it also generates the harvest of our life in the form of all our experiences and endeavours.

Exercise

These are the six points of view that enable us to give form to our life processes:
- Becoming conscious of the problem underlying the process
- Becoming conscious of the desired result

- Becoming conscious of our attitudes in the process
- Becoming conscious of the way we allocate time, or our rhythm
- Becoming conscious of the means we can make available
- Becoming conscious of our core theme in the process

These points of view can help me connect with my 'I' so that I can stay fully awake in my own life processes as I bring them to realisation. A permanent, ongoing exercise is to enter into a tangible life process, to be there and fully engage with it without avoidance. We can enhance the quality of the process by reflecting on our life processes ourselves and in dialogue with others who are involved in it, with the help of these six guiding points of view. Such reflection may enable us to find the right kind of intervention to apply in a process.

PITFALLS
- Striving for perfection at the expense of the vitality of the process
- Ruling out improvisation
- Wanting to make everything predictable
- Trying to fit the other into one's own frame of reference
- Trying to plan a life process as a watertight, self-contained entity and attempting to realise it in that way.

LIVING IN DIALOGUE

Living in processes we meet others. We have conversations, engage in activities together, collaborate and, in doing so, enter into relationship. This encounter, this relationship in the social realm, takes place at various levels of consciousness. In practical life we can quite clearly observe at least three such levels.

THE FIRST LEVEL of conducting dialogue is that of the customer-supplier relationship. We need each other to satisfy our needs. We buy things from each other, perform services for each other, instruct each other. These are encounters with others of which we are not necessarily truly conscious. In the routine of our daily life we make use of each other. In the supermarket I buy my provisions; I put them in my shopping cart and pay for them at the checkout. Often I hardly notice that other people make this process possible for me, help me with it. And yet precisely at this level a real encounter with the other is possible, because the dialogue we enter into here is very tangibly bound to the idea of 'helping each other'.

The train can run if I use it; the physician can heal if I open myself to the treatment; the teacher can instruct if I want to learn. We meet in these processes, in these dialogues, and we can observe the other quite clearly. But usually we are so busy with our own processes that the other escapes our attention. In this sense it is a daily schooling challenge to observe the other consciously in the actual interactions we have together, and to meet there. Whenever such a dialogue repeats cyclically – I regularly shop in that store and meet the same person at the till there – we can build a relationship together and meet each other in that specific situation.

A SECOND LEVEL of dialogue in the social realm can be seen when we work together in an organisation. We are colleagues and together we strive for a common result. We accomplish work processes and meet each other there. Together we are working to make a common idea a reality. Thus we meet each other in a world of goals and policy, rules and procedures, agreements and decisions. Often this is a complicated world in which many people in a variety of roles have to manage to get through one door together. It demands the subtle interaction of an ensemble.

Not only is it important that I am skilled in what I do and am able to deliver quality work, it is equally essential that I meet the other in his capacities and responsibilities. In this world of organised collaboration we are involved in set habits and conventions. The work is performed in a particular way, there is a culture and manner of interacting with each other that was created by our predecessors. The art of dialogue consists here in the ability not to get stuck at the level of routine and convention, but to penetrate through to each other and develop a sense of what this collaboration means for our inner experience.

We can reflect on what values and standards are being addressed in us, how the relationship between us is nurtured. Do we see each other merely as cogs in a system, used to reach a goal? Or do we meet as striving human beings who want to take a step in our own development? To the extent that we are better able to connect our own biography with that of the organisation in which we are working and acting, it also becomes possible to observe and meet the other in the same effort. We enter into an existential connection with each other, and perhaps we even become destiny companions.

Some years ago I founded a new institute for human and organisational development called IMO. I started with three colleagues from my former institute. In the years that followed I met others who decided to join us as colleagues because they wanted and were able to connect their own strongly Christian impulse with that of the IMO community. In addition, this developing IMO institute attracted dozens of members who wanted to create a link between their work in business - as managers, researchers or advisors - with the IMO impulse.

A THIRD LEVEL of conducting a dialogue is the level of personal development, learning from and with each other. In the relationships in our lives we encounter others who are beacons for us in the ways in which they live and give meaning and form to their personal lives. We meet our teachers in a neighbour, a schoolteacher, an author, a colleague at work, our partner, our child. Our inner world is continually stirred up by the events we experience in our lives. We can reflect on these and give them meaning. We do this in interplay with others. Who has something sensible to say about a crucial event I have experienced? With whom do I share, with whom do I learn together?

We engage in a path of inner schooling by learning from, sharing with and mirroring the other. Every problem we meet in life and share with the other opens a door to a new perception and experience of reality. We go our own way in this process, but also meet our life companions there who have connected with our problem. Our problems guide us to other human beings, with whom we can learn and make discoveries.

For many years I spent a week each summer bicycling in the French Alps with a colleague. After the daily ascent of one or more high mountain, followed by a refreshing shower, we would share our intimate reflections on our own lives in the preceding year and then make plans for our next steps. In this way a deep friendship of the heart developed which, however, came to an earthly end with my colleague's untimely death.

Every one of these three levels of dialogue is a source of value creation. At the first level we create economic values. With their products and services people satisfy the needs of other people. It is an art for every person to find his right balance in these things. The needs are endless, and the means to satisfy them are always increasing. Where and how do I set boundaries, where and how do I find a standard that is balanced and responsible? This is a world of sharing with each other, taking care of each other. We can train our consciousness by attentively observing what our contribution is to fulfilling the needs of others, and how others satisfy our own needs.

When we do this we can develop 'excess capacities', creating space for the deployment of energy and the means for initiating meaningful new ventures. We can become conscious of the ways in which we satisfy our needs and how we can do this in ways that are respectful of the environment. This involves continuously making decisions as to what I do or do not want to associate myself with. What do I eat, and where do I purchase that food? Where do I live, and what financial burdens do I take on? And so on.

At the second level we create social values, and also standards. We enter into the world of the other and meet each other there. We find ourselves constantly balancing attending to our own interests and points of view with attending to the space the other needs, and to what the other considers important. This is a process of dialogue in which pictures of and between human beings are constantly being formed, in which judgements are born and shared, and in which decisions and choices are made. This asks each one of us to identify ourselves with the other all the time, while also living truly in ourselves.

We can experience this most vividly in conversation. In speaking and listening together this social element is born and maintained. When we listen to the other, and identify with him or her, we enter into a world of meaning which may not be so well known to us. For a moment we see the world through the eyes of the other. When the other listens to us, we come back to ourselves and can express what is important to us. In this way we can, through each other, develop consciousness of the motives that guide us, and also of the effects of our own actions and behaviour on the other's life situation.

At the third level we create values in knowledge and understanding. Through each other we develop our thinking, feeling and will. In our encounter with the other, in our mutual dialogue, we are confronted with what has developed in us and in the other in the way of living wisdom, living insight and living knowledge. We have developed concepts with which we approach reality and interpret it. With the wisdom we have acquired we give meaning to what we experience. We create meaning in our biography.

By studying together, doing research together, experimenting with new insights together, we create a new world in dialogue with each other and give meaning to this world. Here we meet our fixed ideas, our firm convictions, our life patterns. These can meet and test themselves against the wisdom of the other. The other can ask us questions, and call our attention to the fact that when we have an overriding conviction, its opposite may also need considering. The soul as paradoxical reality becomes mobile through contact with the other who is different.

Through these values we can enhance our lives. Such values are not a self-evident given in divine, natural Creation. Laws and forces reign in Creation, generated by the divine world. These self-evident laws do not reign in the human world of value-creation through dialogue. Here only the laws we create and take in hand ourselves can reign. When I listen to the other, a reality will grow that is different from what happens when I do not listen. When I serve the other and in doing so respond to a real need, a different reality will grow than when I just do my own thing at the expense of the other. We are speaking, therefore, of moral values; I assume a responsibility in interaction with the responsibility of the other.

Exercise

In every customer-supplier situation, in which you are yourself either the customer or the supplier, it is good to focus your attention not only on the current transaction, but also on the human being with whom it is taking place. For instance, we can stop for a moment to notice the person and how he or she is. At the same time we can voice our own judgement of the value of the transaction by reflecting briefly, with the other, on the result achieved.

In every situation where colleagues work together it is good to nurture the process of speaking and listening. We can make sure that all those present are involved in the event, for instance, by asking them a question or requesting their contribution. We can also make sure that our own contribution comes across in a clear and personal manner.

In every learning situation we can give attention to what the other can contribute in the way of vision and experience, and to the way in which this contribution can be included in our own learning process. When we encourage and help each other we make a fundamental contribution to our learning process and, in so doing, to the acquisition of new experiences and insights.

Entering into dialogue with the other is a human path of practice on which we school our personality through the realities we meet on the way. We are enhanced as moral human beings. We participate and assume responsibility in the human creative process. Every one of us forms part of that creativity; we can involve each other in it by seeking dialogue, meeting each other and supporting each other.

PITFALLS
- Wanting to be nice and social but not really engaging with what the other is saying
- Not wanting to take a position so as not to confront the other
- Emphatically pressing a point by repeatedly asserting my own vision or direction
- Wanting to convince the other by argument
- Trying to explain everything in detail to make sure the other understands exactly what I mean
- Seeking to hear and understand the other's whole point of view but only in order to assert my own opinions against it

LIVING IN ONE'S OWN BIOGRAPHY

Everything we think, do, experience and learn, finds a place in our biography. Our biography, as the course of our life, is the all-encompassing story in which our life, and also the life of the communities of which we form part, receives meaning and significance. Our biography is built up from two sources:

- The divine lawfulness that shapes our biography
- The steps we take ourselves on our own initiative.

Regarding divine lawfulness, our biography is formed first of all by the body in which we find ourselves, and which we carry around with us during life. We are living in a body that is built up and decays, and is in a continual process of being created and perishing again. The body grows, takes shape, is nourished, interacts with its surroundings, dies and decays.

In our body we may have to cope with hindrances. The body is not always the perfect organism in which we can express ourselves. For that matter though, we often treat our body as not much more than an instrument. However, to a great extent the body dictates the course and potential of our life, setting boundaries and opening possibilities.

We also have an inner biography, which arises from the steps we take by our own initiative. We are thinking and feeling beings who perform actions and bring things into existence. We form our soul through life and our personality grows in it. We clothe ourselves in the language and culture of our origins, we adopt customs and habits from our educators, we dress ourselves in the trappings of our profession, we school ourselves in the art of life. Thus grows an inner world of convictions and beliefs, of insight and knowledge. We find in ourselves the capacity to take life in hand and clear a path that we can pursue.

In human biography meaning is created in a self-chosen process. Every experience finds its place in our biography and, nourished by reflections on our experiences and perceptions of daily events, joins in the meaning-creating process that we enact every day.

Our biography is not just something that 'happens' to us. As we continue through life we develop an ability to cultivate our biography. When we reflect on the course of our life, considering what we have become in the light of the values we carry within us, our biography begins to tell us its own story. Only in retrospect can we recognise value and discover meaning in what we have experienced. Our biography is our teacher and hands us the material for us to develop our awareness.

When we ask someone to tell us his or her biography we will find that the story is never boring or meaningless. A biographical story is always interesting. We start seeing themes, a purpose in life: destiny becomes visible, can be sensed.

Karma

Our biography leads us into the world of destiny and karma. Questions are living here such as: Who am I? What is the purpose in my life? Do I have my life in hand or does it just happen to me? How do I give meaning to this incomprehensible experience? How do I relate to what happens to the other? We can ask whether our biography was predestined or whether it developed randomly, by chance. We can also wonder what it is that connects us with the other, and what determines this connection. Who are my travelling companions and what have I to do with them?

With biography as karma and life destiny we enter into the mysterious realm of our own life. We will be able to find answers to these questions, provisional answers, if we embark on a reflective exploration of our biography. The path of schooling offered by our biography can be fruitful if we can learn to view it from multiple angles. In other words, our biography may express both a predestined element and also reflect our specific, self-directed choices. Our biography gives us predestined parents and children, to whom we are tied for our entire life, but also the choice to interact with a particular reality and steer it in a different direction.

Our biography reveals a pattern or a particular theme in our life, but also chance events which life bestows on us and which we can gratefully integrate. Within the given context of the book of our life, we are also an open story gradually unfolding. We are part of many communities which form us, yet also a unique personality that determines its own path.

The biography is a unique composition of many life realities. It is nature and spirit, individual and community, human and divine. It is uniquely human.

Exercise

Make a rough sketch of your own biography with the help of the following questions:
- What are the lines of heredity?
- What are the environments that have formed me?
- What is the core theme at work in my life?
- What encounters have I had with people who played, and continue to play, an important role in my biography?
- What was the nature of these encounters?
- What has succeeded as I expected, and what has failed?
- What are the inner and outer obstacles I regularly meet in my biography?

By reflecting on these questions, we can integrate our own biographical experiences more fully into our life, acknowledge their significance and not deny them or close the door on them. In this way we strengthen our own living capital and accord powerful new meaning to our biography. This exploration can be undertaken in dialogue with others.

PITFALLS
- Denigrating yourself, self-condemnation
- Inflating yourself, self-aggrandisement
- Adopting a fixed viewpoint from which to evaluate your biography: 'Sorry, but that's who I am'
- Avoiding difficult situations

The Context of the Path of Schooling in the Social Realm

We have described the basis of the personal path of schooling in ordinary social co-existence as:

- Living with a question
- Living in a process
- Living in dialogue with others
- Living in one's own biography

These four form the basis. The personal path of schooling is enacted in a tangible context. Everyone leads a specific life under specific conditions. What this means will be described as context.

Our lives do not just happen haphazardly. They are always taking place in the here and now, in specific locations and with particular people. And specific thoughts and feelings then stream through us, along with actions: we do something, or omit to do it. Striving to live consciously in these specific conditions is not something that comes easily, for we often like to float past them, escaping in daydreams from all this actual reality. On the other hand, we may dig in our heels and tenaciously hold fast to it, entangling ourselves in the transitory and material aspects of our lives

How do we make sure that we are present, and lead our lives with attention for, and engagement with the here and now, in living connection with what is taking place there?

We all live with inner boundaries or constraints which prevent us from acting with presence of mind in the situations we meet. They keep us from confronting ourselves with what has occurred, and learning from it. These boundaries are apparent in our fears, feelings of alienation, prejudices and rationalisations.

For the personal social path of schooling, which leads to higher consciousness, it is essential to practise being completely present in the specific context. Just as we live in a tangible body, which carries us and which we have to accept for what it is, in the same way we can embrace social reality as a tangible embodiment of our destiny and goals. This social reality is there for my development: it is my teacher, helping me gain insight and take a step forward in my personal development. It is therefore very important to take social reality absolutely seriously, to learn to observe it and accept it, to be present in it with attention, and to receive its lessons and integrate every experience into our existence by attributing our own particular significance to it.

More than anywhere else, social reality manifests in the context of organisations. An organisation can be viewed as the ultimate human creation, in which everything the human being has created is present and working. It is the context in which human freedom can be created by the human being as a unique human value. In this world, organised by human beings, we each adopt our own roles, which make us visible and form us: such as customer or staff member, educator, businessman, priest, driver or nurse. In such roles we can become aware of ourself and enter on a path of schooling. In specific roles in the organised context we begin to participate in the human creative process.

In this way a person can become part of the process of self-governance that enables human interaction to take place. In self-governance the human being becomes a responsible (co-)creator, someone who is able to realise an idea of his own within a work process of his own. In so doing, the human being develops his own soul, which is unique and connects with essential human qualities and values.

LIVING IN ORGANISATIONS

Whereas in the distant past human life took its course in a natural context, today we mostly live in organised contexts. We are co-workers or members of staff in organisations, as customers we make use of countless organisations, and at home we live an organised life. In this organised world we are subject to two explicit forces: a vertical and a horizontal force.

THE FIRST FORCE, the vertical, is built of hierarchical and also functional forces. In organisations we relate to each other along hierarchical lines, and we also perform functions. These vertical forces are controlled with the help of structures and systems. Structures create order in all the functions we perform. Systems help us effectively accomplish the work process in our job. This vertically organised construct is based on the strength of a higher power. Power relationships exist among us; these have to do with our striving to realise goals. Forces have to be pooled and given direction, and in the process we act in service to a cause.

THE SECOND FORCE is horizontal. Here processes of dialogue take place between us. In dialogue with each other we create values and we collaborate. Confrontations also happen here, and we repeatedly have to try to find our relationships with each other anew. We can find our place in the horizontal space once we learn how to move in it. This requires an enterprising attitude, taking initiative. The social process is enacted in the horizontal realm as we establish contact with each other and come into movement together.

Living and working within these two forces we can practise two fundamental orientations. In the vertical we are asked to make ourselves part of a task within a larger whole. We live here in a world of systems in which we accomplish tasks, and can only succeed if we have mastered a skill or trade, and entered into a profession. There we learn a complex of knowledge and skills. We are an administrator or a driver, technician, physician or teacher. We master such specialties and learn to work in them with professional discipline. We can learn to excel in them. In the vertical realm it is very important to be a master in your trade. We do all of this in service to a greater whole. This organised whole generates products or services that have to satisfy the needs of others. In this way we feel completely at home on our materialised earth; we become familiar with the way it works and are able to make our contribution to it.

In the horizontal we are asked to open ourselves. We do so through the questions we are being asked, the help that is wanted from us, the impulse that wells up in us, the idea that occurs to us. We enter into dialogue with others, we explore things, we experiment and try to learn from all of this. We make our way through this organised life, and encounter others with whom we enter into relationships and make connections. In this horizontal space we discover and form new things in a creative manner. We appear here especially as a person; our authentic personality is born and developed here.

In an organisation, therefore, we stand as human beings in the midst of vertical and horizontal forces that can enable us to grow and develop. We can achieve increased responsibility and learn to move more broadly and deeply in a range of situations. In this way we become part of creative communities, and we fulfil our practical life in these.

In ourselves, however, we constantly come up against thresholds or boundaries that hold us back from taking our next steps forward. That is because in the course of our lives we have become part of cultures and customs, of patterns and compelling attitudes. We experience fear of the unknown, and we are concerned with preserving our safety and security. Life, however, always invites us to let go and venture into the unknown. We have the tendency in such a situation to shape a known context around us, so that we only need to respond to what we are familiar with: we have heard it all before, we know it all, it has happened before and therefore we don't need to make the effort to push our boundaries and look for the new. When we abandon that effort, what we experience in our soul is something like a slow implosion. Everything loses value and significance. The experience of meaning diminishes. While every new step can bring a new experience for the child, the adult loses her or his experience of familiar meaning in life.

In organised life we not only meet our own thresholds, but are also strongly confronted by the practical dimensions of space and time. We live in a world of agreements, of constructs. Within these dominant structures of life we seek our path. Am I in the right place at the right time? We see a quality here which we can practise in our lives and learn to master. Moving from place to place through time demands conscious steering of our own life. Dimensions such as rhythm, belonging and staying ahead will play a role in this. In these contexts we have the tendency to let outer contents and structures determine us, and to let systems guide us. We can also orient ourselves to other people, to encounter and dialogue with them, to becoming conscious of the quality of that experience and trying to internalise the meaning we find in that process.

Exercise

Reflect on the question: When did I take an initiative of my own that I actually pushed through to completion in the past few years?
- What was this initiative about?
- Who else was involved with it?
- What steps did I take?
- What were the results?
- Was it appreciated by others?

Regarding the initiative itself we can explore dimensions such as:

- What kinds of resistance did I encounter in myself and in others?
- How did I overcome this resistance?
- What did I learn from it?

We repeatedly encounter the challenge of positioning ourselves either more in the vertical or more in the horizontal. Life asks us find a workable balance between the two. It is a good thing to be conscious of the need to take up a position in the horizontal, since the vertical is always automatically there and tends to predominate. In this sense, in organisations it is a real art to choose as our standpoint an initial orientation to the other person, and enter into dialogue with him or her, before the formal and vertical begins to dominate the situation and what is taking place.

PITFALLS
- Adapting to what is formally demanded without recognising the sense of these demands
- Pursuing your own longings and ideals without connecting them with the longings and ideals of others
- Holding onto outer security and formalities while failing to give attention to, and make room for your own impulse.

LIVING IN ROLES

In the context of organised life we act in roles. For instance, we can adopt the role of staff member, manager, owner, supplier, expert, and many others. In such roles we present ourselves in a specific function and quality. Roles are bearers of responsibility.

First of all, it is most important in social intercourse to actually fill the role that we perform. If we have been given a particular role, it is disturbing to social harmony if we do not actually make that role completely our own. It is like actors playing their roles on stage. Do they play their roles convincingly? It is great to see how an actor puts his personality into a role in which he portrays another person. This can be a fine combination of being himself and yet also being different. In practical life we also play roles and it is a real art to fill the role and play it convincingly.

Let's take the role of the customer. I go to a restaurant and am served. Now and then the waiter, completely at home in his role, asks me if I am enjoying my meal. I can reply with a conventional mumble without disclosing my actual feelings as a customer. If I do that, a little quality of life is lost for both the waiter and for me. How can I enter into dialogue with this waiter in such a way that both of us can best perform our roles? Time and again it is surprising to me to discover how personal engagement and fulfilment of my role as customer helps the other to be more present in his own role. If there is something I am not happy with in my experience in the restaurant, and I communicate this to the waiter, in nine cases out of ten I receive an adequate and pleasant reaction to the problem from the waiter. If I don't feel at home in my role, the other often also does not feel free.

How can I become completely at home in my role? How do I develop role consciousness?

A first step is to really assume the role we have adopted. When we step into a new role, at first it tends to feel a little unnatural. When I want to learn to drive a car, I will feel pretty helpless to begin with. Someone else will help me get into my new role by teaching me the technique, the rules of the road and how to handle difficult situations I may run into. Increased experience will help me grow into the role. In the process, however, things may get into a rut, the automatic pilot takes over. The trick is then to repeatedly develop a new role-consciousness at a higher level.

In this way I can grow from being an apprentice into a professional. There is a personal path of development we have to pursue in really making the role our own. This development is supported by a continual process of acquiring skill. I will move from mere routine to creativity when I force myself to add new meaning all the time to the role I perform. I can remain the same waiter as long as I live, or I can grow to a level where every encounter with a customer foregrounds the process of generating an enjoyable experience for all concerned. I will only succeed in this if I am willing to relate everything I do to this specific situation and this specific individual, so that I do not act out of routine by doing the same old thing each time.

In the dialogue between people in roles there is always room for free creativity. In essence, there is always the possibility of creating a social work of art. This is really the highest art of life. We create a combination of the skills of our trade with social skills, and also with conceptual skills, which together we imbue with the colour of our unique personality. This never becomes boring, it knows no limitations: it always gives us energy and personal development.

Exercise

- What roles do you perform in the organisations in which you work and move?
- It is important to become conscious of these roles and to explore whether you actually fill them
- Are you aware of the roles which others perform, and of the way the interaction is unfolding between the different role players?
- By addressing role consciousness explicitly both in yourself and in others you increase the quality of an event, and you prevent unnecessary complications and uncertainty between different role carriers.

PITFALLS
- Taking over someone else's role
- Inflating your role to unreasonable proportions
- Minimizing your role
- Imitating others too much and being reluctant to show your own personality in your role
- Not learning in the role, but thinking that you know and can do everything already

LIVING IN LEADERSHIP

When we take responsibility for what happens in our personal life, when we want to participate in the organisations with which we are associated and perform a real role, then the door is open for us to take part in the leadership of the organisation without having been formally appointed to a management position. Leadership can be viewed as a process in a community that is enacted among individuals and in which the impulses of that community are being realised in successive steps. This can happen if there are individuals who take on responsibility for this leadership.

We can enter into a world which reaches beyond the boundaries of our personal destiny and our personal circumstances. In this way we can enter into a world called humanity.

Leadership creates relationships

In leadership we interact with other people and, together with these others, realise our strivings and longings. Our leadership, and the way it is practised, has great influence on the way the members of the community can relate to each other and can realise their strivings together. The quality of our leadership finds its expression in the quality of human relationships - which is also determined by our view of the human being, as the basis for the form we give our leadership. For instance, these relationships may be based on power, on guided development, or on research and creativity. Our leadership is a reflection of our active and effective image of the human being and of the way in which we as individuals assume responsibility in that picture.

Leadership is based on the personality of the leader

There is no one best type of leadership; it works according to an entirely personally developed repertoire. The leader works with personally acquired insights and points of view. Our leadership has everything to do with our authentic personality. And the biographical relation between ourselves and the organisation in which we work is of key importance here. How do I as leader, with my personality and value system, fit into what the organisation has built up in the way of values and culture?

Leadership develops as a personal learning process. Reflecting on what we have experienced, sharing this with others, and giving it meaning for ourselves, will help us develop leadership capacity.

Leadership is a community process

Leadership is about people and the way they work together. It develops in a dialogue-type process in the horizontal plane. In this sense it is not functionally determined, but it takes place in a personal and open space. It is a process in which there are many participants, and in which people try to realise their longings and goals. It takes place as a process in which an invitation is extended to participate. People get each other involved in the process of leadership.

The task of leadership is the realisation of development

Leadership is oriented toward the development of the human being and the organization. It mobilises people and processes by orienting itself to the development of human capacities and insights along a path of inquiry and experiment. Along this path the new can enter and be integrated into the human world of experience.

Leadership is a process of giving meaning to our creations, which otherwise have no intrinsic meaning. When I have to fulfil a task in a work situation and have to discipline myself to find my proper place in it, the processes of change and development themselves will challenge me to reflect on the how and why, and to develop my own creative space.

Exercise

The development of personal leadership can be strongly stimulated if we regularly do four small, but far from simple exercises:

- Asking questions of other people we have to work with, which help the other to express himself in a clear manner. When the other can express himself well, a possibility opens up in his soul to wake up for the next step. When our goal is not the satisfaction of our own curiosity and desire to understand, it becomes possible for us to listen at another level: to what moves the other and where he wants to go.
- Sharing with the other what inspires us and forms the basis of the vision informing how we engage with reality. A vision develops; you could say that it is 'talked into maturity'. By sharing your vision with others and entering into dialogue with them about it, your vision begins to develop. It becomes a story that can be told and can also inspire others. By telling our story to the other we create a lively connection with the other, and our own life gradually gains in depth of meaning.
- Daring to take a standpoint of our own in situations that ask for it, and sticking to it at least for a while. Adopting a standpoint is something different from voicing an opinion. A standpoint is something you stand for, which you think is important and can form a good foundation for further progress. We have the tendency to take our own standpoint less seriously than that of others, and therefore to give it up rather easily in favour of that of another; or else, we squarely stick to our standpoint, oblivious of the fact that its effect may be disastrous. The exercise consists in adopting a standpoint that helps the other express himself clearly. This can lead to a deepened insight into what is playing itself out in the situation and what matters.
- Engaging in confrontation with the other because our heart is in the subject under discussion. When we avoid each other and just tiptoe round what does not feel right and does not work well, we do ourselves and others an injustice. We are stuck. By entering into confrontation with the other we practise the social art of concentrating on the essential; in other words, we don't condemn the other, but we address the barrier in ourselves so that we can bring ourselves back into mobility. Confrontation can be painful, but it can also lead to ultimately clearing the air so that everyone can move on and get going again.

By participating in leadership we travel a path of development that connects personal destiny with that of the organised community in which leadership is being practised. Our strengths and weaknesses are tested to the limit. We learn to balance our own interests with those of another, to respect and love not only ourselves, but also the other.

Our individual biography can be interwoven with a vital thread of leadership. There is no need to strive for influential positions in society; leadership is equally needed and effective in small contexts. In the multiplicity of leadership processes our communities develop, and individual people discover their own path of development.

PITFALLS
- Viewing yourself as unworthy to take on responsibility
- Distrusting what someone else sees in you
- Playing for power and wanting to outdo the other
- Manipulating the other, and also your own self-image

LIVING IN THE SOUL

When, as I have described, we fully assume our roles in organised contexts and participate in leadership, we develop our soul to a higher level of consciousness.

We have already characterised the soul as our thinking, feeling and will. These are the three soul forces that form our inner world, in which we come to consciousness. The soul is engaged in a continual process of transformation, and this leads to metamorphosis in our thinking, feeling and will towards a higher level of consciousness.

OUR THINKING transforms itself from functional thinking about content to creative thinking in processes. Whereas we initially develop an intellectual capacity capable of comprehending the complex world of our organised existence, step-by-step the soul develops a higher form of thinking. This is a kind of pictorial thinking – we could call it 'meta-thinking' - through which we can gain insight into the way in which we approach content, and school our thinking processes. In intellectual consciousness we are limited to thinking in terms of cause and effect. That is what we learn in school. We are capable of following a particular line of reasoning. When we move into organised life we begin to discover the limitations of this kind of thinking. It does not really work in social contexts. It brings us no further than making factual statements, explaining the background or category of something. We can rise to a higher level of thinking if we attain to heart thinking, which can encompass diversity, complexity and relationships. Things can exist side by side with each other, in mutual relationship. Then we will also see how something in a state of dis-relationship can be brought into movement.

Heart thinking is thinking in paradoxes, in polarities, in terms of forces rather than fixed products or entities. The way to develop this thinking is by schooling our observation. Instead of rushing on into abstractions we stay with an observation. By continual observation we discover that things do not simply exist as they are but that they metamorphose over time. Everything is continually being transformed into a higher state of being through a process of death and rebirth. We process our ongoing observations into living thinking when we constantly ask ourselves questions and are surprised by the transformations we observe.

FEELING also develops to a higher level of being. Then feelings don't just surge up and down in our soul, aroused by the countless experiences we have in our lives, but are sensed inwardly as qualities in the soul. Empathy comes into being: through feeling we become able to identify with the other person or situation. This demands a purified feeling life. We engage in this process of purification by working on our feelings through higher thinking. We become conscious of different levels of feelings.

Then feelings no longer appear as experiences that come and go in a passive, fluctuating way, but they transform into a capacity to sense what is living in the other. It is a refining process. Initially our feelings are unrefined and can manifest in violent emotions. Gradually, during the purification process, our feelings become refined into organs of sensibility that give us a living relationship both with the other person and with events in our own life. We develop a higher form of experience and perception, in which we allow ourselves and everything else to exist as it is, in our and their own qualities.

WILL, which lives in us initially as a propelling force and pushes us ahead to realise our urges and desires, is turned into creative deed by our higher thinking and purified feeling. A deed is performed not only out of an erratic inner impulse or desire, but is undertaken consciously because it responds to what the situation demands. We can bring our will into relationship to that of others. In this way our will power develops into a healing power. We learn to let our individuality speak in our will, and can thus enter into true encounter with the other. We learn to enact free deeds that can work fruitfully and creatively in the social reality in which we meet each other.

In this way our soul forces of thinking, feeling and will become higher elements in us so that we create a new quality in ourselves. The beautiful thing about this is that our soul then enters into communication with all kinds of creative forces that seek to influence the work of humanity. We become aware of these forces. We encounter good forces, but also evil ones; we find support and meet opposition. Rather than being caught up in these forces, we learn to communicate with them. We can meet them and even invite them to participate in the process we are involved with. It becomes an act of inclusion rather than exclusion.

Thus we learn to include people of all kinds in our processes: we involve them and take them along without having to give up or lose our own individuality. In this way we create a higher form of community. Despite all our differences, together we become a new destiny community in which we can connect with each other at the level of spiritual freedom.

Having now considered the foundation of the personal path of schooling in practical social life, and directed our attention to the context of this path, let us consider a third element: the path of schooling we can pursue.

The Path of Schooling of Body, Soul and Spirit

When we embark on this self-chosen path of schooling in the social realm we will find out that it isn't a rose-strewn path. We will have to work at it. An important part of this work is learning. Learning to master something involves training ourselves and making it our own through practice. It is a path of learning and practice in daily life.

The child clearly shows us this, but adulthood does not mark the end of it. We are not so conscious of this in the hustle and bustle of every day while dealing with a multitude of problems and questions. Whereas the child acquires skills in a natural way, learning to stand, walk and speak, the adult has to design or create processes enabling him or her to enter upon this path of learning.

The human being, with his three elements of body, soul and spirit, faces the challenge of embarking on a threefold path of schooling.

I will therefore now describe a path of schooling for each of these three, which anyone can take as a path of schooling in the social realm.

- I can school the body through nourishment and exercise
- I can school the soul through dialogue
- I can school the spirit through reflection and contemplation

When someone decides to embark on a personal path of schooling the fruits of this schooling will be become apparent in human creative work. As we develop to a higher level of consciousness, the community we co-create will then also radiate a higher quality of consciousness.

The Schooling of the Soul

The path of schooling of body, soul and spirit in the social realm is a path of development. Besides nourishing and taking care of body, soul and spirit to prevent them succumbing to the 'violations' of daily life, these elements of ourselves must also be brought into development so that they can carry the individual's inmost core, the 'I', in a living way.

THE BODY exists in a permanent process of death and rebirth. It is constantly dying and being formed anew. In the first half of life the body is built up in an expansive process, and made progressively stronger; in the second half the forces of wear and tear increase and we try to preserve our bodily strength as long as possible.

THE HUMAN SPIRIT awakens during life, and can unfold increasingly as life progresses. Provided that this spirit is given the chance to manifest, it comes to ever stronger expression in the authentic personality.

BODY AND SPIRIT are the result of a divine process of creation and form part of the lawful progress of creation. They have their own inner laws and belong to the earthly and spiritual worlds. These two worlds are part of our lives, and we can treat them with respect. The realms of body and spirit are also home to other beings, such as gods, animals and plants – some physically embodied, others not. The human being is interrelated with all of this.

THE SOUL is the unique creation of the life a person leads, and engages in a continual process of metamorphosis and intensification. We can observe this in the transformations we pass through through in the course of our biography. Our thinking, feeling and will are formed during life, and nourished by our physical and spiritual qualities.

In the light of this picture, we can see that we ourselves have to nurture body and spirit. They exist, and can be either more or less effective and present, depending on the nature of the care they receive. We ourselves however repeatedly form the soul anew. The nature of the process in which this happens forms and creates the soul. In this sense the soul is a being living in dialogue: first, she comes into being in dialogue between body and spirit, and then she develops her form and content in dialogue with other souls.

On the one hand, the soul shows what she has inherited from her parents and ancestors, while on the other hand the soul-forming environment becomes visible in what she acquires and experiences from people and events around her. And last but not least, the authentic personality, the 'I', is revealed in the soul and manifests there as unique individuality.

The body

When we want to nurture the body we can cultivate two points of reference:

- BODILY FITNESS. All kinds of processes are taking place in the body. The body is not just matter, but above all process. It streams and breathes. Bodily processes unfold in intimate interaction with each other; and it is an art to maintain the body in a state of such fitness that these processes can be optimally balanced with each other.
- THE BODY MUST BE CARED FOR IN ACCORDANCE WITH ITS OWN NATURE. It has to be washed and cleaned, fed and refreshed.

In order to make these two points of reference our own we have to pay attention to nourishment and exercise of the body. These are two conscious deeds that can have great impact on our physical state.

Through nourishment we can give the body the substances it needs to realise its processes. One good premise here is moderation, meaning that nourishment is given and absorbed in right measure. Over- or underfeeding disturbs the equilibrium. But we must all also attend to the quality of nourishment. Some bodies are allergic and have trouble tolerating certain foods. And foods vary greatly from one part of the world to another. Each of us absorbs nourishment individually, and in this process we can maximise our capacity to be conscious of what and how much nourishment nurtures the body and keeps it fit.

Besides nourishment exercise is important. It supports physical processes and helps the body to regenerate. For instance, half an hour's walk every day is good for the body. Movement, sometimes accelerated movement, will stimulate the body to better absorb oxygen and nourishment into the blood. This improves the quality of the blood, the carrier of life.

What is good for one person is not necessarily good for another. All kinds of advice we get for physical fitness and good nourishment, for instance, cannot be taken at face value. What counts is our own observation as to how one thing or another works in our bodies. By paying attention to nourishment and exercise we enable the body to do a better job for us.

The spirit

When we want to bring the human spirit to manifestation so that it can shed light on everything that happens in and to us, we can again choose two points of reference.

- THE SPIRIT APPEARS IN ITS GREATEST STRENGTH WHEN FOCUSED. The spirit lives from the world of ideas and seeks to realise in earthly existence the ideas with which it can connect. When the spirit is wandering about unconnected with what can be considered real and essential, it will not be able to manifest. But the spirit is also dependent on the observations we make. For instance, when we live with a question we become better able to observe phenomena which can help us make progress with this question. In the absence of any question, we may observe many things, but they don't speak to us. The spirit is then not able to nourish inspiring ideas or give meaning to our experiences.

- THE SPIRIT SHINES WHEN IT IS CLEAR. Clarity is related to truth. We live in images of the world, of ourselves and others, which may be murky because we have filled them with a multitude of elements completely unrelated to what is essential. We are overwhelmed by emotions or driven by desires, and will then view the world, ourselves and the other in distorted images. To manifest in its true colours, the spirit needs clarity.

These two points of reference - focus and clarity - can become effective if we choose two premises as the foundation of our lives:

- BEING PRESENT IN THE HERE AND NOW. When we try to live in the here and now, and be present, we can experience presence of mind. We are completely connected with what is and what is going on. Also, the future and the past can have their own presence in us – can also live in the here and now.

    Presence of mind can be practised and cultivated as follows. First of all, try to be ahead of what is happening. If we are always present before something begins, we increase our chances of 'arriving'. Being late creates problems: we are still involved with what has gone before, and have difficulty entering into what and who is present before us.

    In addition, the spirit can come into presence by entering into a relationship with another person, by making contact, by dialogue. No floating away, no insistence, no dismissing of another, but connecting with who is there and what is taking place. This is what the spirit needs in order to work within a situation. Then, bringing things to a balanced conclusion and taking one's leave can open up the situation so that a new step becomes possible.

- A SECOND PREMISE IS OPENNESS. The spirit can be closed, but it can also open up. This openness comes into being in the encounter with what is different in the other. The spirit is eager to learn and know. It seeks contact with different realities. Openness also means revealing yourself to the other. Something perhaps shines out from you that can inspire the other, and makes an encounter possible. The spirit comes to fullest expression if in everything I do I direct myself to the 'I' of the other, to his or her personality, and if I am not too distracted by everything the soul of the other is revealing to me.

The soul

When we want to form and develop the soul, we have to enter into the world of dialogue which we ourselves create in interaction with others. The human soul is not an isolated entity but always connected with other souls. The mother and her child, colleagues with each other, the members of a sports team, the customer and his supplier – in reality the human being always stands in dialogue with other people. The soul is also always connected with what has happened, what is perhaps about to happen, what could happen and what should not happen. The soul is an inherent part of our paradoxical reality of human creativity. She lives in polarities and contending forces, in inner and outer worlds, representations and judgements, longing and goals. As such the soul is a mirror of human society and of the human being's authentic nature. These two stand in their own relationship to one another.

The human being can adopt two points of reference for the development of the soul:

- The first is liveliness. When the soul is ensnared in static patterns, in fixed habits and iron convictions, she will shrivel, becoming increasingly intolerant and tending to close herself off. However, when she follows every wind and lets herself be seduced by everything and everyone, she will fragment and evaporate. The soul must be in balance between rigidity and dissolution. When she achieves this balance she will be experienced as lively. The other will notice the lively presence of such a person: something shining out that works on others and appeals to them.

  The soul can practise liveliness by always being ready to enter into new situations, and by always taking time to reflect on her experiences so she can gain significant insights. Moreover, when the soul meets something or someone she has met before, she can try to look for nuances in the other, for what is different and new. For instance, in a long relationship we can continually try not to pigeonhole the other but to experience them with fresh surprise.

- THE SECOND IS CONSCIOUSNESS. The soul is a playful organ that hopes to sound all sorts of different notes of experience and enjoyment. The shadow side of this is that our neighbour's grass is always greener than our own, and the soul is never completely satisfied. This can lead to frustration.

  The soul has the capacity to develop higher consciousness. The quality of our thinking, feeling and will changes if we are willing to school ourselves to live consciously. This schooling of consciousness can be done through exercises.

For instance, THE THINKING AND CONCENTRATION EXERCISE.

- Try to keep your thoughts focused on a simple object such as a pen, without being distracted, and don't allow all kinds of other thoughts to crowd in.

THE FEELING EXERCISE is also an excellent one:

- Each day try to find something good, something positive in every situation.

Then there is THE WILL EXERCISE:

- Perform a small, unnecessary action at the same time every day - such as taking your wallet out of your pocket and putting it back again.

This strengthens your capacity to act independently of any outer, determining influence.

In addition, the review exercise is helpful for attending to your life more consciously and creating meaning in our lives. It also helps you let go of the day's events and fall asleep!

- Look back over your day in the evening and try to see yourself in your actions, in order to find those moments when you acted with consciousness and those when you did not. You can also consider how you might act differently in future, but without any self-condemnation or regret. All such exercises should be progress-oriented.

Two qualities of life will help us bring these points of reference into being:

- LIVING WITH ATTENTION. Accomplishing every action, but also every thought, with attention will lead to greater quality of life. The other person will immediately notice whether you are present and act in a situation with attention or not. Are you unobservant or attentive? For instance, as a patient, doctor, nurse, parent or provider of services. Do you give your attention fully to interpersonal dynamics?

    Attention can be practised. If we can control our haste, if we can extend our fascination with our own life to interest in what is different in the other, then we can begin to hear the inner voice of attention. Every situation in life offers us this possibility; it is a permanent exercise.

- ENTERING INTO CONNECTION. If we do not want to pass the other by – and pass ourselves by in the process – then the quality of entering into connection is of the essence. How do I connect with the other, with the work and the task, with myself? Connection demands that one person seeks the other. This requires us to enter into movement. We have to overcome our inner barriers and step out of our own world. Connections demand faithfulness. To whom and what am I faithful? Is this the faithfulness of a dog, or do I have an individualised connection? Entering into connection also entails making choices. I cannot connect with everyone and everything. If I choose A, that does not mean B is gone. But if I unite with one person, I may have to leave another behind. In connecting with each other our souls can school and form themselves through the mutual relationship.

The Personal Social Path to Higher Consciousness

In today's world, in which we lead organised lives, and in which we have been uprooted from natural and spiritual sources that nourish our body and spirit, we may ask how we can nurture our soul, and the soul of the other in the communities of which we form part. In the past, human beings were embedded in the communities to which they belonged and in which they played specific roles. In our time, no longer so firmly entrenched in our communities and roles, we can free ourselves from these ties and connections. In taking our leave from them we can seek out our own communities and roles in daily social life.

It is my premise that human beings can school themselves in caring for the soul by the way they deal with the social questions they encounter in their lives. In this process we meet opposing forces which become apparent in the resistance we meet in ourselves and others, as well as in the pitfalls in which we are trapped during our efforts to take a step forward on our developmental path.

Becoming familiar with these opposing forces, naming them, and learning to deal with them will strengthen us as we develop greater consciousness and individuality.

In conclusion I will outline three fundamental adversarial forces which stand in our way:

- COMPLACENCY, SELF-SATISFACTION. We are full of ourselves, filled with our ideals and longings, and do all we can to make our life as pleasant as possible, so we can bask in satisfaction. We would like to lead our lives with as much ease, and as much support from others as possible. We constantly appeal to others to support us and are disappointed if they are not willing to do this. We have the best intentions and want to do what is right, but are not willing to open our eyes to the actual consequences of our own actions and behaviour. We invariably draw on all sorts of arguments and statements to justify our conduct.

- Displays of power – of the power we want to exercise in order to impose our will on life. We are critical of others, we see their constant failings and the incapacities; we see how they cannot and will not respond to the demands put on them. In the meantime we believe that we ourselves are completely under our own control and fully oriented to satisfying the demands we have created. Overlooking in myself what does not accord with my self-image, I oppress the other who tries to dispute my ideas. I view the other as subordinate to the goal I set, and in self-interest I use the other to attain my own goals.

- Exclusion and sabotage of the other. Everything that does not fit in with my ideas must be excluded and dismissed. Whatever does not respond to my idea, does not contribute to my interests, has to be removed. There is only one valid idea, one dogma to be obeyed, one truth to be worshipped. Everything else either has to fit in with this or must be dismissed. Sometimes this requires violence. In such situations the individual is expected to subject his destiny to the destiny of the community. I sacrifice myself to the higher ideal, and also expect this from others. Whoever does not go along with it is excluded.

These adverse forces work in and occupy our souls. In deciding to enter upon a path of schooling in the social realm, we become able to grow towards a consciousness that allows us to deal with these adverse forces in ourselves in relation to the other. This can enable us to learn to remould these forces into effective powers that help us to make real the common human ideal of freedom, love for the other and ourselves, and respect for everything that is different.

Afterword

In this book I have outlined a possible path of schooling to develop higher consciousness in the practical context of daily social co-existence. My intention is to help us all participate in a consciously experienced social reality, and at the same time seek our schooling in this reality. We can make a conscious choice here to use our own potential to become individuals who live consciously and think freely, on the path towards increasing maturity. This process can be reinforced by our own personal efforts at self-schooling, to make us more receptive to what is spiritually enacted in our inner world.

About the Author

Reflections at the age of sixty five years (b.1947)

He is a writer
Adriaan Bekman is a writer for over 30 years on books about organisation development, change, leadership and self-management. Cape-town, his first novel was published in 2011. He also wrote *Changing with Soul* (2011) and *Organisations with Soul* (2011)

He is a musician and a composer
Playing saxophone in jazz-bands, he formed his own group *Language of the Soul*. He made a stage performance of this using his musical compositions, movement, pictures and anecdotes. This was performed in Germany, Brazil, Chile and the Netherlands. He plays Irish folksongs and slow airs on the violin with friends in his Irish cottage.

He is a painter
Adriaan paints images of the soul. They are colourful images exploring the expression of the soul in colours and movement.

He is a scientist
He wrote a doctoral thesis on Changing organisations: the client at the centre of our attention. He published the methodology of the evidential in scientific magazines. This method offers a unique way of exploring social issues.

He is an entrepreneur
Adriaan founded IMO 'instituut voor mens en organisatieontwikkeling' in 2005. He leads this international group of 14 consultants that works in Europe and South America. They help organisations to lead change. IMO has 65 IMO network members. He created centres for horizontal leadership in Brazil, Germany, The Netherlands, Finland and Italy. In these centres there are research-groups on the questions of organisation development and leadership. They organise master classes of one year on leadership and on change leadership consultancy.

He is an adviser
He is well known as a Dutch leading consultant. Was twice nominated for the Dutch book prize for consultancy. He was a leader in the Association for Social Development, a worldwide network of OD consultants working out of Bernard Lievegoed's impulse.

He is a philosopher
Adriaan studied 2500 years of philosophy on the questions of God, the soul and freedom. He just finished a 500 page book on the philosophy of organisational life.

He is a professor at Stenden University in the Netherlands
With his knowledge group of 35 people he researches issues on leadership, sense making and community. Students can follow his minor programme on the art of horizontal leadership.

He is a coach
Adriaan coaches CEO's of public and private companies in Europe and South America.

He is a life artist
He reshaped a cottage and a farmhouse in Ireland and made them into centres for music and art. He travels the world giving lectures and inspiring talks to all kind of people on the art of conscious living.

He is a father and a grandfather
He is a father of two artistic daughters and grandfather of two grandchildren.

He is married
He is married to Jutta Hodapp, who was born in the Black Forest.

The focus of Adriaan in this wide-ranging passionate exploration of life-themes is always the same: 'How can I enter into the soul and how can we meet the other'. Words like 'process, dialogue and biography' play a central role in this question.

He searches for the impulse of Christ in human life .

Bibliography

Adriaan Bekman, *Zelfmanagement – in een druk bestaan*, Assen 1999

Adriaan Bekmen, *De mens als bron voor leiderschap*, Assen 1997

Arthur Koestler, *Scum of the Earth*, Gollancz, London, UK, 1941

Bernard Lievegoed, *Scholingswegen*, Zeist 1992

Kees Locher and Jos van der Brug, *Workways: how to build an enterprising life*, Hawthorn Press, Stroud , UK, 1997

Rudolf Steiner, *How to Know Higher Worlds*, Steinerbooks, Hudson NY 1994

Rudolf Steiner, *Verses and Meditations*, Rudolf Steiner Press, London 1961

www.het-imo.net

OTHER BOOKS FROM HAWTHORN PRESS:

Springboard, 7th Edition
Women's development workbook
Liz Willis, Jenny Daisley

Springboard helps you do what you want to do in your life and work. It gives you the ideas and skills to take more control of your life and then gives you the boost in self-confidence to start making things happen.

Springboard is for all women at work. Whether you are in full time or part time employment, considering employment, wanting to return to work, just starting out, or approaching retirement. *Springboard* helps you to be the best you can be!

"A comprehensive women's development programme."
The Guardian

336pp; 246 x 189mm; paperback; ISBN: 978-1-907359-28-6; £35.00

Navigator, 3rd Edition
Development Workbook for Men
James Traeger, Jenny Daisley, Liz Willis

This workbook is for all men at work or seeking work: for men on their own, men in relationships and men as fathers. This third edition of the *Navigation Development Workbook for Men* has been extensively revised and updated based on the experiences of thousands of men who have successfully completed the programme and the changes that have taken place globally.

"*Navigator* is one way men can develop a much needed new sense of identity at work, as well as a better balance between home and work."
The Independent

www.springboardconsultancy.com
320pp;246 × 189mm; paperback; ISBN: 978-1-907359-01-9; £30.00

Social Ecology
Applying Ecological Understanding to our Lives and our Planet
David Wright, Stuart Hill, Catherine Camden-Pratt,

Social Ecology addresses the question of how to apply ecological understanding to every aspect of our lives. The 27 contributors, all of whom have directly or indirectly contributed to the teaching of social ecology, share their experiences in this 'coming of age' anthology of keynote articles.

"An excellent anthology giving a superb and exciting overview of the emerging and vitally important field of social ecology. We need to implement the ideas in this book as a matter of utmost urgency if we humans are to have a viable future on this planet."
Dr Stephan Harding, Schumacher College, UK. Author of *Animate Earth: Science, Intuition and Gaia*

336pp; 234 × 156mm; paperback; ISBN: 978-1-907359-11-8; £25.00

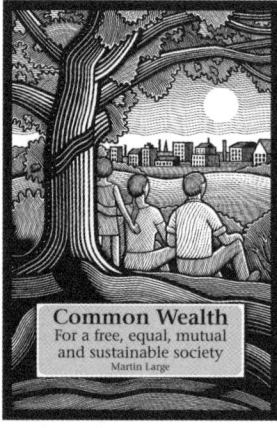

Common Wealth
For a Free, Equal, Mutual and Sustainable Society
Martin Large

Just when 'the market' nearly took over all areas of life, the credit, climate and democratic crunches came along, challenging us to rebuild a society that works well for all. Common Wealth asks, 'How can we build a more free, equal, mutual and sustainable society?'

"Brings us bang up to date and tackles difficult questions from the perspective of a man who has made new ideas work. In fact, he has inspired me to re-think much of what I do."
Alastair Sawday, from the Foreword

256pp; 234 × 156mm; hardback; ISBN: 978-1-903458-98-3; £15.00

Where on Earth is Heaven?
Jonathan Stedall

This book is a response to the author's young son once asking, 'Where on earth is heaven?' What lies behind this question has motivated Jonathan Stedall's career as a distinguished documentary director. His films about Tolstoy, Gandhi, Jung, the educational and curative work inspired by Rudolf Steiner, have been milestones on his journey of exploration; so too the insights of Pierre Teilhard de Chardin and Ralph Waldo Emerson.

Jonathan Stedall explores challenging questions about living and dying, looking and seeing, heaven and earth, and our human potential. He draws on forty years film-making experience, largely at the BBC, working with inspired artists, scientists and writers like John Betjeman, Laurens van der Post, Fritz Schumacher, Bernard Lovell, Malcolm Muggeridge, Alan Bennett, Fritjof Capra, Cecil Collins, Ben Okri and Mark Tully.

592pp; 234 × 156mm; hardback; ISBN: 978-1-903458-90-7; £20.00

The Storyteller's Way Sourcebook for Inspired Storytelling
Sue Hollingsworth and Ashley Ramsden

Everyone can tell a story, but to tell it well you need a certain set of skills. Whether you're starting out or want to develop your storytelling expertise, this book is an essential guide.

Use it to tell stories for entertainment, teaching, coaching, healing or making meaning. It contains a wealth of stories, exercises, questions, tips and insights to guide your storytelling path, offering time-tested and trusted ways to improve your skills, overcome blocks and become a confident and inspirational storyteller.

256pp; 228 × 186m; paperback; ISBN: 978-1-907359-19-4; £20.00

Ordering Books

If you have difficulty ordering Hawthorn Press books from a bookshop, you can order direct from our website, **www.hawthornpress.com** or from the following distributors:

UK
BookSource
50 Cambuslang Road
Glasgow G32 8NB
Tel: (0845) 370 0063
email: orders@booksource.net
www.booksource.net

USA
SteinerBooks
PO Box 960, Herndon
VA 20171-0960
Tel: (800) 856 8664
email: service@steinerbooks.org
www.steinerbooks.org

CANADA
Trifold Books
PO Box 32, Guelph
Ontario, N1H 6J6
Tel: (519) 821 9901
email info@trifoldbooks.com

AUSTRALIA
Footprint Books
1/6a Prosperity Parade
Warriewood
NSW 2102
Tel: (02) 9997 3973
email: info@footprint.com.au
www.footprint.com.au

NEW ZEALAND
Ceres Books
Ceres Enterprises Ltd
121 Carbine Road
Mt Wellington, Auckland
Tel: (64) 9574 3356
email: info@ceresbooks.co.nz
www.ceresbooks.co.nz

Hawthorn Press

www.hawthornpress.com